REVELATION
A SELF-STUDY GUIDE

Irving L. Jensen

MOODY PRESS

CHICAGO

Contents

Introduction   4
1. Background of the Book of Revelation   7
2. Interpreting Revelation   16
3. Survey of Revelation   27
4. John's Vision of Christ (1:1-20)   36
5. The Seven Churches (2:1–3:22)   44
6. Visions of God and the Lamb (4:1–5:14)   52
7. Seals of Judgment (6:1–7:17)   64
8. Trumpets of Judgment (8:1–9:21)   77
9. The Little Book, Two Witnesses,
     and the Seventh Trumpet (10:1–11:19)   91
10. The Woman, Dragon, and Two Beasts (12:1–14:20)   102
11. Bowls of Judgment (15:1–16:21)   116
12. The Fall of Babylon (17:1–18:24)   123
13. Final Judgment (19:1–20:15)   130
14. Eternal Home of the Saints (21:1–22:21)   141
The Geography of Revelation   150
Bibliography   151

Introduction

If the message of Revelation was relevant in the times of its original readers, around A.D. 100, its relevance today is amplified a thousandfold. For Revelation is a book about the final years of world history, which laymen as well as theologians agree must be upon us. Your study of this important book of the Bible can be one of the most exciting experiences of your Christian life as you gain new perspectives concerning God's timetable for His universe.

This manual is intended to be a *companion* in your Bible study, not a *substitute* for it. Three of its main purposes are:
1. to encourage you to study for yourself
2. to offer guidance on paths of study, through questions and similar directions
3. to help you maintain a momentum and continuity in your study, right up to the end of the book (chap. 22)

Parts of Each Lesson:

1. *Preparation for study*—This is like a baseball player's "warm-up" before going to bat. Involved here are such things as learning background and reading related Bible passages.
2. *Analysis*—This is the heart of all Bible study. Many questions are included in each lesson. Also, work sheets (analytical charts) for recording observations, and survey charts for views of context appear throughout the manual.
3. *Notes*—Much of this information cannot be derived from the passage itself, hence its inclusion here.
4. *For thought and discussion*—This part of the lesson stresses application of the Bible text. If you are studying in a group, the subjects mentioned here are recommended for extended discussion.

5. *Further study*—These are supplementary studies. Continuity in the lessons does not depend on your completing this phase.

6. *Words to ponder*—Tarry at the end of each lesson over the thought expressed.

Suggestions for Study:

1. Let the Bible speak for itself. When an interpretation is suggested by the manual, check it out with the Bible text.

2. Look for the main underlying parts of each of John's visions. Develop an "instinct for the jugular."

3. Keep large context in mind as you analyze the smaller parts.

4. Don't get bogged down in difficult details. You can always return to these at a later time.

5. Always keep a pencil in hand to record observations. *Jot it down!*

6. Use at least one other Bible version in addition to your basic study text, for comparison of readings. (The King James Version is the basic version of this self-study series.) Also, a good commentary will be especially helpful for the difficult parts of Revelation.

7. Have healthy attitudes in Bible study. Some important ones are:

a. A dependency on the Holy Spirit for enlightenment and understanding

b. A believing heart: As one has rightly said, "Unbelief is the greatest enemy of prophecy"

c. A teachable spirit: "All Scripture is . . . profitable for . . . instruction"

d. An obedient heart: willingness to apply the truths learned

Suggestions to Leaders of Study Groups:

1. Determine how much of each lesson may be adequately studied at each group meeting. Assign homework accordingly. Remind your class to write out answers to all questions.

2. Start the meeting on time; close on time. (Extended discussions, visiting, etc., may continue after the class meeting is over.)

3. Stimulate discussion during the class meeting. Encourage everyone to participate, including the asking of questions. Some can do more; some can do less; but all can do some.

4. If possible reproduce on a chalkboard or poster paper the major charts of the manual, for easy reference in the class discussion. Remember the importance of the "eye gate" for teaching.

5. Devote the last part of your meeting to sharing the spiritual lessons taught by the Bible passage. This should be the climax of the class session.

6. Make the class continually aware of the supernatural dimensions of the events of Revelation. If doubt is expressed over any of the fantastic prophecies of the book, refer the discussion ultimately to a recognition of *who God is*. This is basic to *what He does*.

7. You are the key to the atmosphere of the class. Aim to keep it relaxed, frank, sincere, interesting, and challenging.

Lesson 1

Background of the Book of Revelation

The unique setting of the actual writing of Revelation foreshadows the action and color of the text. In this opening lesson we will be studying things about the book, such as where it originated and when. Such a study takes the book out of the "stranger to me" category, and gives us confidence, momentum, and interest as we proceed in our analysis of its text.

I. AUTHOR

Four times the author is identified by name as John (1:1, 4, 9; 22:8). Read the verses, and note how John relates himself to others. Both internal and external witness is strong in identifying this John as the beloved apostle, author of the gospel and the three epistles.[1] It is interesting to note that John does not name himself in the gospel or in his epistles, whereas he does so here. This may be because the very nature of prophecy calls for identification and credentials of the author.

II. DATE AND DESTINATION

John probably wrote this book around A.D. 96, at the end of the reign of the Roman emperor Domitian (A.D. 81-96). Domitian banished John to the isle of Patmos (see map) because of his Christian stand (Rev. 1:9). In such trying circumstances the apostle received visions from God, which he recorded on a scroll.

God directed John to send his inspired manuscript to seven churches in western Asia Minor (Turkey). Read the list of churches in 1:11, and observe on the map how the order of the

---

1. For more information about the biography and character of the apostle John, see *John* (Chicago: Moody, 1970) in this self-study series.

list was determined. There were other churches in Asia Minor at this time, such as the church at Colosse, to whom Paul wrote Colossians. But in the sovereign design of God the *designated* local recipients of this original manuscript were only the seven listed churches.[2] The larger intended audience of the book, however, was all people, everywhere, of all centuries (read 2:7, 11, 17, 19; 3:6, 13, 22).

III. HISTORICAL SETTING

Study chart A for an overview of the historical setting of the book of Revelation.[3]

Observe the following:
1. The change of area of John's ministry from Jerusalem to Asia Minor (particularly the city of Ephesus).
2. The age of the local churches of Asia Minor when Revelation was written.
3. An increasing intensity of imperial opposition to Christianity.[4]
4. John's writings, separated from the other New Testament books by a period of fifteen to twenty years, were given to the Christian church to complete the body of divine Scripture.

IV. JOHN'S EXPERIENCE OF INSPIRATION

The book of Revelation is the written record not of wild dreams, but of dramatic God-sent visions given to one of God's servants. John says he was "in the Spirit on the Lord's day" (1:10) when he heard and saw the things which he was commanded to write down. The man John appears from time to time as an active participant in the narrative of the book (e.g., 5:1-5), but for the most part he is only the recorder of the visions he beheld. In a sense the details of the visions, especially those concerning future events, were beyond John's ability to understand completely. The reality of Bible prophecy is not dependent on full comprehension by the prophet himself.[5]

2. More is said about this in the study of chapters 2 and 3.
3. For a very informative discussion of the status of Judaism and Christianity in the Roman Empire, where Revelation was written, consult Merrill C. Tenney, *Interpreting Revelation*, pp. 20-27.
4. The worst of persecution was yet to come for Christians, when John wrote Revelation. This made the ominous message of Revelation all the more relevant.
5. For example, the Old Testament prophets were not fully aware of all the details involved in the fulfillment of their prophecies about Christ's first coming.

8

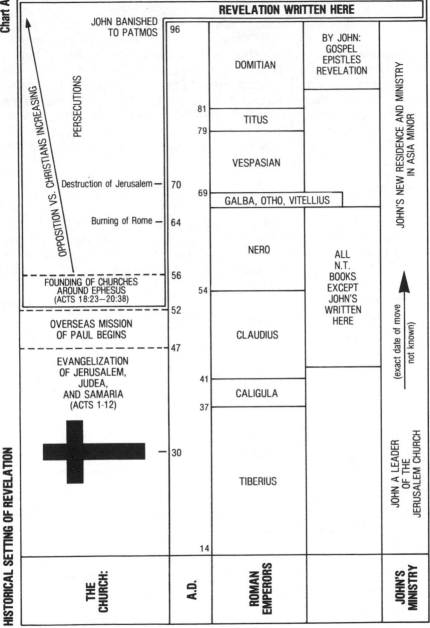

Chart A

HISTORICAL SETTING OF REVELATION

REVELATION WRITTEN HERE

THE CHURCH:	A.D.	ROMAN EMPERORS		JOHN'S MINISTRY
JOHN BANISHED TO PATMOS	96	DOMITIAN	BY JOHN: GOSPEL EPISTLES REVELATION	JOHN'S NEW RESIDENCE AND MINISTRY IN ASIA MINOR
	81	TITUS		
	79	VESPASIAN		
Destruction of Jerusalem —	70			
	69	GALBA, OTHO, VITELLIUS		
Burning of Rome —	64	NERO	ALL N.T. BOOKS EXCEPT JOHN'S WRITTEN HERE	(exact date of move not known)
	56			
FOUNDING OF CHURCHES AROUND EPHESUS (ACTS 18:23—20:38)	54			
	52	CLAUDIUS		
OVERSEAS MISSION OF PAUL BEGINS	47			
EVANGELIZATION OF JERUSALEM, JUDEA, AND SAMARIA (ACTS 1-12)	41	CALIGULA		JOHN A LEADER OF THE JERUSALEM CHURCH
	37			
	30	TIBERIUS		
	14			

OPPOSITION VS. CHRISTIANS INCREASING

PERSECUTIONS

9

V. TITLE OF THE BOOK

Our English title *Revelation* is taken from the first word of the book (read 1:1). The Greek word is *apokalypsis,* which means the unveiling or uncovering of something previously hidden. A common illustration is that of a basket, with a lid on it, containing an unknown item. To "reveal" would be to take the lid off the basket, letting the item be seen at that time. Read the following verses where the words *reveal* and *revelation* or their equivalents appear with that meaning: Galatians 1:12; Romans 8:18; 1 Corinthians 1:7; 2 Thessalonians 1:7; 1 Peter 1:7, 13; 4:13; 5:1; Daniel 2:19, 22, 28, 29, 30, 47; 10:1; 11:35.

VI. THEME

The opening verses of Revelation (read 1:1-13) identify this basic twofold theme of the book: (1) revelation of the Person, Jesus Christ; (2) revelation of instruction for Christians.[6] As the book unfolds, these specifics appear over and over again.

CHRIST IN THE BIBLE   Chart B

OLD TESTAMENT	GOSPELS AND ACTS	EPISTLES	REVELATION
HIS MINISTRY PROPHESIED	HIS MINISTRY INITIATED	HIS MINISTRY INTERPRETED AND APPLIED	HIS MINISTRY CONSUMMATED AND HIS CLAIMS VINDICATED
(MESSIAH)	DEATH AND RESURRECTION	——————————————————————▶	GLORY (KING)

A. Revelation of the Person Jesus Christ

1. *About Him.* Christ is the Judge, Redeemer, and triumphant King. Revelation is the climax of the Christolcentric theme of the Bible, shown in Chart B.

6. The genitive "of Jesus Christ" in 1:1 grammatically is either an objective genitive (i.e., Jesus is the one revealed), or subject genitive (i.e., Jesus is the one revealing). The intention of the passage is probably both, that is, revelation *about* Christ and revelation *from* Christ.

2. *From and by Him*. This in word (e.g., 1:2; 2:1-3:22) and in deed (e.g., 5:5).

B. Revelation of Instruction for Christians

1. *Prophecy*. Most of the book predicts events future to John's day, especially those of the end of time. And most of that predictive section describes divine judgments of sin; the last few chapters describe the glorious triumphs of Christ culminating in a thousand-year reign (20:1-6) and in an eternal heaven (chaps. 21-22).

2. *Historical perspective*. Revelation shows world history of the end times as God views it, and describes His application of justice to both individuals and nations. World history is sovereignly controlled by God, and will culminate in the Person of Jesus Christ (read 11:15).

3. *Doctrinal instruction*. If Revelation were the only book of the Bible, we would still have much light on the vital areas of truth, such as man, sin, angels, Satan, judgment, salvation, church, worship, heaven, hell, and God the Father, Son, and Holy Spirit.

4. *Spiritual application*. Exhortation is another aspect of the theme of Revelation, made prominent in the book. As an example, read 1:3 and note the three words "readeth," "hear," and "keep."

VII. PURPOSES

Revelation is addressed to believers (God's "servants," 1:1), although its message is a loud and clear warning to unbelievers as well. It is a book "for a troubled age . . . in which the darkness deepens, fear spreads over all mankind, and monstrous powers, godless and evil, appear on the stage of history."[7]

The book encourages Christians to persevere under the stress of persecution, in hope of justice which must ultimately triumph at the enthronement of Jesus Christ as King of kings and Lord of lords. As one has written, "Whenever the Church is threatened by destruction, and faith is dim and hearts are cold, then the Revelation will admonish and exhort, uplift and encourage all who heed its message."[8] Christians living in John's day, under the growing threat of imprisonment and even death of emperor Domitian, found comforting refuge in the message of Revelation, even as have persecuted Christians of all the ages since then.

7. Wilbur M. Smith, "Revelation," in *The Wycliffe Bible Commentary*, p. 1492.
8. Martin Kiddle, the *Moffat New Testament Commentary, Revelation*, ed. James Moffatt (London: Hodder & Stoughton, 1941), p. xlix.

The book of Revelation also warns Christians against the treacherous swamplands of apostasy with their tragic toll, and it appeals for faithful allegiance to Christ. The letters of chapters 2 and 3 especially emphasize this.

Revelation does not aim to give all the prophetic details of the end times. Nor is the full program of church history spelled out. Enough details are recorded to (1) describe the crucial events (such as the great white throne judgment, 20:11-15); (2) portray the large movements and trends of world history; and (3) teach spiritual principles underlying God's sovereign plan. These are the things that the student of the book of Revelation should inquire into.

VIII. APOCALYPTIC TYPE OF WRITING

Revelation is prophetic in character and apocalyptic in form.[9] Here are some of its major features as apocalytic literature:[10]

1. mainly eschatological (*eschatos*: last times)
2. written during times of persecution
3. visions abound
4. style generally figurative, with an abundance of symbols

IX. RELATION TO OTHER SCRIPTURES

The book of Revelation is the natural climax and conclusion to all the other Scriptures. Genesis is the book of beginnings ("In the beginning," Gen. 1:1); Revelation is the book of consummation ("for ever and ever," Rev. 22:5). And, as Revelation 22:13 boldly asserts, Jesus is the key to all of history, for He is "Alpha and Omega, the beginning and the end, the first and the last."

A. Relation to the Old Testament

Allusions to Old Testament imagery and prophecy appear throughout Revelation, though there are no direct quotations as such. Of its 404 verses, it has been observed that 265 contain lines

---

9. Other apocalyptic books of the Bible are Daniel, Ezekiel, and Zechariah. The apocalyptic form of Revelation, because it was so different from the other New Testament books, had much to do with the delay in this book's being accepted as canonical by the Eastern church. The Western church, however, early recognized its divine inspiration.

10. In many ways Revelation differs from noncanonical apocalyptic writings, such as in its overall optimism, moral urgency, and identification of authorship.

that embrace approximately 550 Old Testament references. As one writer has said, "This book is the work of a Jew saturated with Old Testament prophecy, under the guidance of a word of Jesus and the inspiration of God."[11] A few examples of allusions to the Old Testament are listed below. Read the passages involved.

OT	Revelation	OT	Revelation
Jer. 51	chap. 18 (Babylon)	Dan. 7:13; Zech. 12:10, 12	1:7
Dan. 7, 8	chap. 13 (2 beasts)	Dan. 7:9, 13; 10:5	1:14
Zech. 4	chap. 11 (olive trees and candlesticks)	Dan. 10:6; Ezek. 1:24	1:15
		Isa. 11:4; 49:2	1:16
Dan. 12:7	12:14 (time periods)	Isa. 44:6; 48:12	1:17
Ex. 19:6	1:6	Isa. 38:10	1:18

B. Relation to the New Testament as a Whole

Review Chart B, which shows some of this relationship. Spend more time thinking about how Revelation is a vital complement to the other New Testament books.

C. Relation to the Olivet Discourse
(Matt. 24:1-25:46; Mark 13:1-37; Luke 21:5-36)

This would be a good time for you to read this prophetic discourse of Jesus concerning the end times and His second coming. Keep its prophecies in mind as you study Revelation. Some expositors consider the Olivet Discourse to be the key to an understanding of the prophetic calendar of Revelation.[12]

D. Relation to John's Other Writings

John was given the happy privilege of writing about the gospel of LIFE in three different kinds of Scripture. These may be compared thus:

11. See Smith, p. 1495.
12. See Wilbur M. Smith, *A Treasury of Books for Bible Study* (Natick, Mass.: Wilde, 1960), pp. 235-42, for an extensive comparative study of the two Scriptures.

The Fourth Gospel (biography):
  Eternal LIFE for the Christian
Three Epistles (letters):
  Divine LIFE in Christian living today
The Revelation (visions):
  Victorious LIFE now and for eternity

It was not by coincidence that the last three inspired sentences penned by John were on such a victorious note:

Surely I [Jesus] come quickly.

Even so, come, Lord Jesus.

The grace of our Lord Jesus Christ be with you all (Rev. 22:20-21).

REVIEW QUESTIONS:

1. Recall what you have learned about this book's author, date of writing, and destination.

_____

_____

2. Describe the state of the Christian church in the Roman Empire when Revelation was written.

_____

_____

3. In your own words, identify the theme of Revelation. Make a list of its main subjects.

_____

_____

4. In what ways was Revelation relevant to the needs of Christians at the turn of the first century?

_____

_____

5. Do you think the original reader understood all the details of Revelation? Do you think John did? Is the book more understandable today in the light of history now past? Explain.

_____

_____

6. What are some of the main characteristics of Revelation as an apocalyptic writing?

_____

_____

7. What are the distinctive contributions of Revelation to the canon of Holy Scripture?

_____

_____

8. What do you anticipate learning in your study of the text of this last inspired book of God?

_____

_____

Lesson 2

Interpreting Revelation

Many of Revelation's prophecies are as difficult to interpret as they are fascinating to read. But this difficulty need not cause frustration if the student will take the right approach to the book. The main purpose of this lesson is to suggest ways and attitudes of approaching the book of Revelation, so that you will not get bogged down in those kinds of details and difficulties that inevitably bring discouragement and defeat. Also included in the lesson is a brief description of the main schools of interpretation of Revelation.

I. STEPPING-STONE APPROACH

When tackling any Scripture involving difficult portions, the wise approach is to go from the known to the unknown, from the clear to the unclear. This might be called a stepping-stone approach, which follows two principles:
1. Start with the basics.
2. Proceed in the correct order.
Let us apply this to our study of Revelation, involving *procedure* and *content*.

A. Order of Procedure

The correct order of procedure in Bible study is this:
1. Observation (What does the text say?)
2. Interpretation (What does it mean?)
3. Application (How does this relate to man?)
As shown in the following diagram, observation is basic to your study of Revelation.

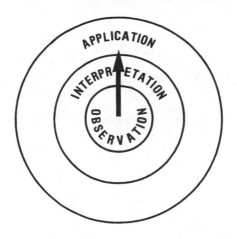

You cannot interpret correctly unless you observe correctly. And correct applications depend on sound interpretations. Spend much time analyzing what the text says, and be content to postpone the phase of interpreting until you have a good grasp of what each verse, paragraph, and chapter says. This principle is applied in Lesson 3, where in our survey of the entire book of Revelation we will be making only observations, leaving interpretations to a later time. (Note that the survey Chart F records no interpretations as such.)

B. Order of Content

Even in following the correct order of procedure shown above, you still have the problem of difficult passages in Revelation. The most satisfactory solution to this problem, again, is to be found in your *order* of study. Here we are talking of order and content—as stated earlier, moving from the clear to the unclear, from the known to the unknown. The following diagram represents such an order.

1. The unshaded circles represent that which is generally clear in Revelation; the shaded circle represents the ambiguous, complex, obscure portions.

2. The arrow represents the order of study, as to overall content, which should be followed in each passage of Scripture.

3. Note that the central core is *Doctrine and Exhortations.* These parts of Revelation (e.g., the letters to the seven churches of Asia, chaps. 2-3) are the easiest to understand. Such clear doctrines and exhortations are found even in the difficult prophetic sections of the book (e.g., the doctrine of redemption in chap. 14).

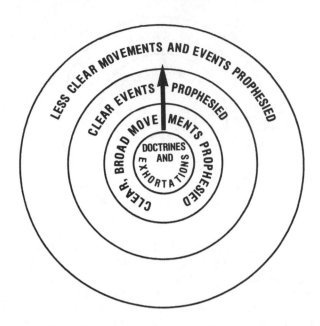

In the diagram: LESS CLEAR MOVEMENTS AND EVENTS PROPHESIED / CLEAR EVENTS PROPHESIED / CLEAR, BROAD MOVEMENTS PROPHESIED / DOCTRINES AND EXHORTATIONS

In your first study of Revelation you would do well to major in this area of content as a solid groundwork for studies in the prophetic aspects. Happily, the clearest passages are also among the most important.

4. The remaining three concentric circles represent the prophetic content of Revelation, in descending order of clarity. As you study this book, discover first of all the clear, broad *movements* of the prophecies (e.g., Where will world history culminate?). Then identify the clear *events* (e.g., the great white throne of 20:11-15). What remains to be interpreted are the less clear movements and events, shown on the diagram as shaded. These admittedly constitute a fair amount of Revelation. The best solution to this problem is to let that which is clear (unshaded on the diagram) shed light on the unclear (the stepping-stone approach). You will want to resort to outside sources for assistance here, but even these are best used after you have done your own independent study in the areas of clarity.

II. IMPORTANT THINGS TO RECOGNIZE

Weigh carefully each of the following statements, which are intended to help you approach the book of Revelation correctly:

1. As prophecy, the book of Revelation is didactic (e.g., teaching doctrines) as well as predictive. Compare this with the twofold ministry of Old Testament prophets: forthtelling *and* foretelling.

2. As the last book of the Bible, it may be expected to teach about the consummation of world history in the last times.

3. Although it is a book of visions, the visions describe real events in actual history, most of which were future at the time of writing, and are still future (cf. 1:19).

4. The book of Revelation is profitable for readers of all centuries. "Blessed is he that keepeth the sayings of the prophecy of this book" (22:7). Its prophecies of the last times have been relevant to all generations, since the date of the last times has never been revealed by God in Scripture. In view of this, the book becomes increasingly *more* relevant with the passing of each generation.

5. As in all books of the Bible, that which is clear is essential.

6. The Holy Spirit may be looked to for help in understanding this vital part of Scripture. One of His ministries is to guide the believer into all truth, even concerning "things to come" (John 16:13)

III. SOME LAWS OF INTERPRETATION TO FOLLOW

A. Law of Plain Sense

"When the plain sense of Scripture makes common sense, seek no other sense; therefore take every word at its primary, ordinary, usual, literary meaning unless the facts of the context indicate otherwise." This approach, besides being the most sound one, raises fewer problems than the opposite procedure, that of taking everything as figurative unless there is proof to the contrary. In some passages of literal interpretation may be *allowable* but not *preferred* over a figurative one, as the student sees it. This is what gives rise to differences of view even among students of the same school of interpretation.

B. Law of Balance

Even when the first law (above) is followed, much of Revelation is to be interpreted figuratively. The book abounds in symbols, for instance. The law of balance appeals for the avoidance of the two extremes in interpreting a symbol, which are: (1) viewing symbols only generally and (2) forcing detailed meanings to every part of a particular symbol.

C. Law of Setting

Let the language and historical setting of John's first century throw some light on his choice of words and on the very visions he was given. For example, we would not expect to read such a modern phrase as "atomic fallout" in the book, though that may be involved in the actual fulfillment of one of his visions.

D. Law of Context

Immediate context is always an important determinant in the interpretation of a Bible verse. For Revelation, the more distant context of parallel Old Testament passages should be taken into account (e.g., the book of Daniel).

E. Law of Structure

Do not force any system or outline upon the book. Look for *prominent* clues to structures. Let the book stand as it was originally written, whether its structure be chronological, topical, a combination of both, and so on. Also, allow for such things as backtracking in the prophetic sections, where the author may choose to amplify what he has first recorded in general outline.

F. Law of Prophetic Perspective

In the prophetic sections, just as in Old Testament prophecy, the author may not necessarily foretell every important event of the future. John was given visions of *certain* epochs and events, represented by the mountain peaks of this diagram:

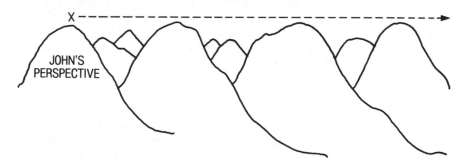

Divine selectivity was the determinant of inspiration here.

IV. THE SYMBOLISM OF REVELATION

As noted earlier, Revelation is filled with symbols, such as numbers, colors, animals, stones, persons, groups, places, and actions. Three categories of symbols appear in the book:[1] (1) those interpreted in the text itself (e.g., 1:20); (2) those to be interpreted in the light of Old Testament usage; (3) symbols of no apparent biblical connection. Because of limitation of space in this manual, no further description of symbols is given here. Different symbols are treated specifically in the course of the analyses of the lessons that follow. When such examples appear in a lesson, watch how interpretations are arrived at. It would be very helpful to you at this point to consult a few commentaries for their discussion of this subject.[2]

V. SCHOOLS OF INTERPRETATION

Basically, there are four different schools of interpretation of the book of Revelation. These are shown on Chart C. Observe on the chart where each view places each of the twenty-two chapters of Revelation. This is one of the best ways to see the major differences between the schools. Observe the following concerning the different views:

1. The symbolic view interprets Revelation only as a series of pictures teaching spiritual truths. It sees no prophecy of specific historical events in Revelation. The first and last chapters of Revelation are a clear argument against such a static view.

2. The preterist view sees all of Revelation fulfilled in the first century, with eternal destinies taught in the last two chapters. This view suffers much of the anemia of the symbolic view.

3. The continuous-historical view applies Revelation prophetically to all the centuries since the time of Christ. Only chapters 19-22 foretell events after Christ's coming. Proponents of this view differ widely in identifying historical events prophesied in chapters 4-18. Some typical interpretations are shown on the chart (e.g., the mighty angel of chap. 10 is the Reformation).

4. Of the four schools, the futurist position sees most of Revelation (chaps. 4-22) as prophetical of the *end times*.

1. See Merrill C. Tenney, *Interpreting Revelation*, pp. 186-93, for a discussion of this subject.
2. Recommended sources are Tenney, *op. cit.;* John F. Walvoord, *The Revelation of Jesus Christ*, 25-30; *The Wycliffe Bible Commentary*, pp. 1494-95; and J.P. Lange, *Revelation*, pp. 14-41. Lange's discussion is the most extensive of the three sources.

THE FOUR MAIN SCHOOLS OF INTERPRETATION OF REVELATION Chart C

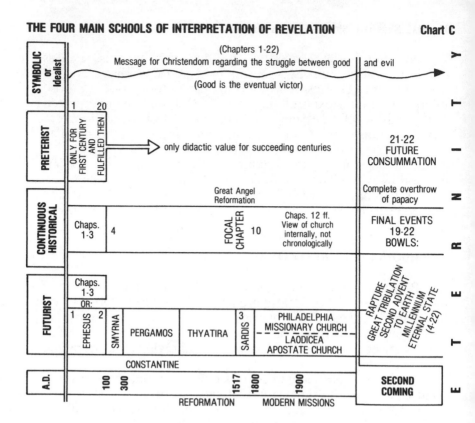

5. There are two types of futurists: (1) those who hold that the seven churches of chapters 2-3 represent periods of church history up to the rapture (as shown on chart); and (2) those who hold that chapters 2-3 are intended not to be prophetic but descriptive, of the churches in John's day, with chapter 4 beginning the predictive section. This view also sees the seven letters as descriptive of local churches of all ages, up to the end times.

VI. MILLENNIAL VIEWS

The Millennium passage of 20:1-6 is the classic passage giving rise to three different viewpoints of the "thousand years."[3] Here are the main tenets of these schools:

---

3. The word *millennium* represents the Greek phrase translated "thousand years" (in Rev. 20:1-6).

A. Premillennialism

Christ will come to the earth *before* the Millennium begins, to rule the world with His saints, for a literal 1,000 years. Satan is bound, as to activity and power, during this time.

B. Postmillennialism

The second coming of Christ is at the end of (post, *after*) the Millennium. This Millennium is a period of time (not necessarily a literal thousand years) of blessedness, prosperity, and well-being for God's kingdom in the world. According to this view we are now living in the Millennium. This school has relatively few adherents today, for the simple reason of the apparent intense activity of Satan throughout the world.

C. Amillennialism

There is no (ā-) literal reign of Christ on this earth for a literal 1,000 years. A common view is that the Millennium is a spiritual reign of Christ with His saints in heaven at the present time.

Chart D shows in a general way how each of these millennial schools views the scope of the entire book of Revelation.

It should be noted here that the Millennium passage of Revelation (20:1-6) constitutes a very small proportion of Revelation because the book does not purpose to give a detailed description of the church and Israel in the end times.

MILLENNIAL VIEWS OF REVELATION Chart D

Revelation	1-3	4-18	19-22
Premillennial	First-century churches; (possibly representative of historical stages)	generally same as futurist school	—Christ returns to set up a literal millennial kingdom —great white throne judgment —new heaven and new earth
Postmillennial	First-century churches	generally same as continuous-historical school	—second coming of Christ —last judgments —new heaven and new earth
Amillennial	First-century churches	symbolic, preterist, or continuous-historical school	—second coming of Christ —last judgments —new heaven and new earth

VII. THE SECOND COMING OF CHRIST

When John wrote Revelation he recorded words of Christ stating clearly that He would return to this earth. Among these references are:

2:25 "Hold fast till I come."
3:11 "Behold, I come quickly."
22:20 (after the visions end at 22:5) "Surely I come quickly."

There are references in Revelation that show that Christ will be on this earth when the particular vision being recorded is fulfilled. For example, in chapter 19, Christ, identified as the "Faithful and True" (v. 11), is shown in combat against the kings of the earth (v. 19). The normal question to ask concerning such passages is, Where in Revelation does Christ return to this earth, fulfilling His promise that He would so come back? In your studies of the book you will want to find an answer to this question.

The premillennialist position is that there are two phases to Christ's second coming, as shown on Chart E.

PREMILLENNIALISM'S TWO PHASES OF CHRIST'S SECOND COMING   **Chart E**

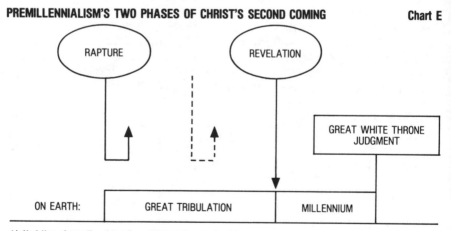

(dotted line shows the view of a midtribulation rapture)[4]

The first is the rapture, when Christ comes to the "air" above this earth to "catch up" deceased and living saints (1 Thess. 4:14-17). The second phase is His coming to the earth, sometimes known as the revelation, with His already raptured saints, to con-

---

4. There is also a postribulation view which places the rapture at the end of the Tribulation, followed immediately by Christ's return to the earth.

quer the hosts of Satan at the end of the great Tribulation, and to inaugurate His millennial reign. Normal questions to ask here also are, Can two phases of Christ's second coming be seen in Revelation? If so, where? Keep this in mind for later study.

Although the second coming of Christ is an important teaching of the book of Revelation, detailed events attending it, such as the rapture, are noticeably absent. On this, John F. Walvoord writes,

> The rapture as a doctrine is not a part of the prophetic foreview of the book of Revelation. This is in keeping with the fact that the book as a whole is not occupied primarily with God's program for the church. Instead the primary objective is to portray the events leading up to and climaxing in the second coming of Christ and the prophetic kingdom and the eternal state which ultimately will follow.[5]

This observation will be confirmed in your survey study of Revelation, which is the subject of the next lesson.

REVIEW QUESTIONS

1. What are some basic attitudes to have in studying the book of Revelation?

_____

_____

2. What approach to the book will minimize the frustration over what appears to be many difficult details?

_____

_____

3. Describe the six laws of interpretation given in this lesson.

_____

_____

_____

4. Name and describe the different schools of interpretation of Revelation. According to which view is most of Revelation still future?

_____

_____

5. Walvoord, p. 103.

5. Why is the future of this world, up to its end, so important to any generation?

_____

_____

Lesson 3
A Survey of Revelation

The rule "Image the whole, then execute the parts" is a must for an effective, sound study of Revelation. So before we begin to analyze Revelation chapter by chapter, we need to get an overview or skyscraper view of the book. Here we are interested primarily in (1) the prominent features of the book; (2) important related items; and (3) a survey chart that will represent the underlying structure of Revelation. In this lesson the focus is consistently on *observation*—what does the text say? The phase of *interpretation* —what does the text mean?—will be included in the studies of each of the remaining lessons.

I. PROCEDURES OF SURVEY

A. First and Second Readings

If something is prominent in a book, it will usually be noticed in the first survey readings of that book. So the thing for you to do first is to scan the entire book of Revelation in one sitting, not reading every word as such, but glancing at its content in a general way. Return to the book for a second, less-hurried scanning. Then record on paper some of your general impressions of the book. For example, How much of the book is action? How much is description?

B. Opening Paragraph Phrases as Clues

One effective way of viewing the overall movement of the book is to observe the opening phrases of most of its paragraphs. Do this for each of the references shown below, recording the phrase as shown in the three examples:

1:1 The Revelation of Jesus Christ	12:13
1:4 John to the seven churches	13:1
1:9	13:5
1:12 And I turned to see	13:11
1:17	14:1
2:1	14:6
2:12	14:14
3:1	15:1
3:7	15:5
3:14	16:1
4:1	16:8
4:6	16:17
5:1	17:1
5:6	17:6
5:11	17:15
6:1	18:1
6:12	18:11
7:1	18:21
7:9	19:1
7:13	19:9
8:1	19:11
8:7	19:17
9:1	20:1
9:7	20:4
9:13	20:7
9:20	20:11
10:1	21:1
10:8	21:9
11:1	21:15
11:4	21:22
11:15	22:1
12:1	22:6
12:7	22:16

What does this study reveal concerning the general contents of Revelation?

C. Assigning Chapter Titles

Go through the book again to identify the main subject of each chapter. Record these chapter titles on the following survey chart work sheet (examples are shown):

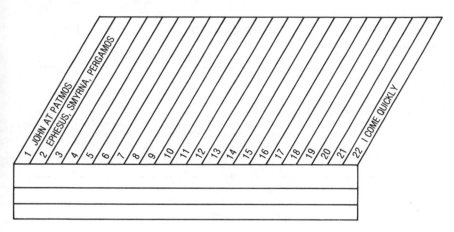

II. IDENTIFYING THE PROMINENT SUBJECTS AND FEATURES

Write out your own list of prominent subjects that you have observed in your survey readings thus far. Some of these may appear in the selected list given below.
1. Groups: What chapters record the following groups:
   letters to the churches; judgments of seals; trumpets; bowls? Record these on your work sheet.
An interesting outline by Wilbur M. Smith is built around groups in Revelation, in this symmetrical pattern.:[1]

3 chapters—letters to seven churches
3 chapters—seven-sealed book
3 chapters—seven trumpets
3 chapters—darkest hour of world history
3 chapters—seven vials
3 chapters—Babylon and Armageddon
3 chapters—Millennium, last judgment, New Jerusalem, eternity

1. Wilbur M. Smith, "Revelation," in *The Wycliffe Bible Commentary, p. 1501.*

2. Songs: Mark in your Bible all the songs of Revelation. What is the usual theme of the songs in the book?

3. Time references: The phrase "after these things I saw" appears often, suggesting an orderly *sequence* in the course of the book. Do you see any other patterns?

4. Christ: Christ appears in various forms, such as a lamb. Tenney's outline shows the overall ministry of Christ in the book:[2]

1:1	1:9	4:1	17:1	21:9	22:6
Christ Communicating	Christ in the Church: The Living One	Christ in the Cosmos: The Redeemer	Christ in Conquest: The Warrior	Christ in Consummation: The Lamb	Christ Challenging

5. God: Much about God can be learned from Revelation. The name "God Almighty" appears eight times. Read these verses: 1:8; 4:8; 11:17; 15:3; 16:7, 14; 19:15; 21:22.
6. Other prominent subjects: angels (76 times in the text), wars, sin, Satan, beasts, thrones, the number seven, church, Temple, kingdom, and geographical names.
7. Did you observe in your survey reading the recurrence of certain phrases? Compare your observations with this list: "I was in the Spirit" (1:10; 4:2; 17:3; 21:10); "and I saw" (more than 40 times); "lightnings and thunderings and voices" (4:5; 8:5; 11:19; 16:18); "It is done" (16:17; 21:6); "Blessed is [are]" (1:3; 14:13; 16:15; 19:9; 20:6; 22:7; 22:14).

III. OBSERVING IMPORTANT RELATED ITEMS

In analysis of a short passage, one constantly looks for relations between particular words and phrases. In survey of the entire book, this inquiry is just as vital. Here are a few examples of the latter:

2. Merrill C. Tenney, *Interpreting Revelation*, p. 33.

1. Songs usually appear before judgments. Can you suggest a possible reason for this?

_____

_____

2. Judgments do not appear until chapter 6. How are chapters 1-5 introductory to the judgments?

_____

_____

3. How do chapters 21 and 22 differ from the general content of chapters 6-20?

_____

_____

4. How are the judgment series (seals, trumpets, and bowls[3]) related to each other? Observe, for example, that the seventh seal (8:1) constitutes the whole series of trumpets; and the seventh trumpet (11:15) constitutes the whole series of bowls. Is there a seventh bowl? (See chap. 16.)

_____

_____

_____

5. Observe the *reappearance* of certain subjects toward the end of the book. Read the following pairs of verses, which illustrate this principle of anticipation.

Early Reference	Later Reference	Early Reference	Later Reference
1:5; 3:14	17:6; 20:4	2:27	19:15
1:5	17:14; 19:16	2:28	22:16
1:6	20:6	3:4, 5, 18	19:14
1:8	21:6; 22:13	3:5	13:8; 17:8; 20:12, 15; 21:27
2:7	22:2, 14		
2:11	20:6, 14	3:12	22:4; 21:2, 10

3. The word "bowls" is used for "vials" throughout this manual.

6. How would you compare these three divisions of Revelation on the basis of your study thus far: chapters 1-5; 6-20; 21-22? This is an important exercise in your survey study.

_____

_____

_____

IV. CONSTRUCTING A SURVEY CHART

One of the clearest ways to show the structure of a book's content is by use of the survey chart. This especially applies to a book like Revelation where there are so many parts, movements, and complex relationships. One of the advantages of a survey chart is that one can see the many parts of the book *simultaneously*, for comparison purposes. (Note: If you choose to construct your own survey chart, begin with the work sheet used earlier in this lesson. Help in constructing a survey chart is given in the author's *Independent Bible Study* and *Acts: An Inductive Study*.[4]

Chart F represents the main structure of Revelation. Use it in the course of your study for these two purposes:

1. Seeing the context—It is an important rule of Bible study that one should always be aware of the *forest* while he is walking among the *trees*.

2. Adding other observations—superimpose on the chart from time to time your own observations of the text.

Note that there are no interpretations as such on the survey chart. Only the facts of Revelation are represented (either by words of the Bible text or by descriptive equivalents).

Observe the following concerning the survey chart:
1. There are three main divisions of Revelation. What are they?

_____

_____

Why is a main division made at chapter 6? Why one at chapter 21?

_____

_____

Note also the outline that divides the book into two parts: "things which are;" "things which shall be hereafter." These phrases

---

4. Irving L. Jensen, *Independent Bible Study* (Chicago: Moody, 1963), pp. 106-13; and *Acts: An Inductive Study* (Chicago: Moody, 1968), pp. 43-54.

THE REVELATION OF JESUS CHRIST

KEY VERSES: "THINGS WHICH ARE, AND THE THINGS WHICH
SHALL BE HEREAFTER," 1:19.

ALSO: "THE REVELATION OF JESUS CHRIST . . ." 1:1.

2 KEY WORDS: LAMB (29 times), THRONE (44 times)

Some interpretations of rapture: 4:1
11:11 ff.
14:1 ff.; 14 ff.
19:9 ff.

THE TIME IS NEAR 1:3

I AM ALPHA 1:8

AND OMEGA 22:13

SURELY I AM COMING SOON 22:20

THINGS WHICH ARE

THINGS WHICH SHALL BE HEREAFTER

INTRODUCTION

JUDGMENT

GLORY

VISION BEGUN CHRIST IN MIDST

SEVEN CHURCHES

THRONE IN HEAVEN

BOOK AND THE LAMB

SAINTS SEALED

THE LITTLE BOOK

TWO WITNESSES

WOMAN AND DRAGON

SEA- AND EARTH-BEAST

3 ANGELS

MOSES SONG OF MOSES AND LAMB

WINE PRESS

SEVEN BOWLS

HARLOT AND BEAST

FALL OF BABYLON

HALLELUJAH CHORUS

Judgment of Satan

Millennium

Great White Throne

NEW JERUSALEM

IMMINENT RETURN

MESSAGES

SONGS

SEALS

SONGS

TRUMPETS

BOWLS

SONGS

7th seal (8:1)

7th trumpet (11:15)

CHRIST COMES TO EARTH

GREAT WHITE THRONE

SONGS

TRUMPETS

I AM COMING SOON
22:6

NEW HEAVEN

CHRIST IN MIDST

GOD ON THRONE

PARTIAL JUDGMENTS

MORE SEVERE JUDGMENTS

PREPARATION FOR FINAL JUDGMENT

CONSUMING AND FINAL JUDGMENTS

MIL-LEN-NIUM

CHRIST AND GOD VS. THE HOSTS OF EVIL

CHRIST AND GOD ON THRONE

1 2 3 4 5 6 7 8 9 10 11 12 13:11 14:6 14:14 15:5 16 17 18 19 20 21

33

come from 1:19, where the two time references are brought out clearly in this translation: "Write, then, the things you see, both the things that are now, and the things that will happen afterward" (TEV[5]). Why is the division point for this outline made at chapter 4?

As of John's day, what proportion of Revelation was history yet to be fulfilled? Compare also 1:1.

2. For clarity's sake, a proportionately larger space is devoted on the chart to the three series of judgments than to the other events. This trio (SEALS ⟶ TRUMPETS ⟶ BOWLS) is the unifying element of the judgment division (chaps. 6-20).

3. Observe on the chart how the seventh seal and seventh trumpet unify the series of judgments. Does this suggest a *forward movement* in the chronology of the book?

4. Note also that there is a parenthesis or interlude between the seals and trumpets and between the trumpets and bowls. How many chapters are involved in each parenthesis?

5. Observe the progression: partial judgments—more severe judgments—consuming and final judgments. This progression will be studied more closely in the later lessons.

6. The "great white throne" judgment is the final judgment for mankind. There are no final judgments cited in Revelation beyond this.

7. Observe on the chart how *songs* appear before each event or era of judgment.

8. God is on the throne *before* the conflicts of the judgments division and *after* those conflicts. There is no question as to who is the victor.

9. Note the key verses, key words, and title of Revelation as shown on the chart.

5. *Today's English Version.*

10. Quantitatively, most of Revelation is about judgment and conflict. What does this reveal concerning one of the purposes of Revelation?

_____

_____

11. Study the survey chart until you are familiar with the general structure of Revelation. When you feel you have mastered this, then move on to the analytical lessons that follow.

Lesson 4

Revelation 1:1-20

John's Vision of Christ

The opening chapter of Revelation describes the setting and introduces the theme of the Bible's last volume. Catch the spirit and see the scope of this opening passage and you will get off to a good start in your analytical studies.

I. PREPARATION FOR STUDY

1. If you have not already done so, locate on a map the isle of Patmos (v. 9) and the seven cities of "Asia" (v. 11).

2. For background to some of the verses, read the following: Exodus 19:6; Daniel 7:9, 13; 10:5, 6; Zechariah 12:10; John 19:37; Ezekiel 1:24; Isaiah 44:6; 48:12; 1 Peter 2:5, 9; Matthew 24:29-30.

3. Recall the historical and political setting of John's exile, which you studied in Lesson 1.

4. You may want to read this chapter in a modern version first, to enliven phrases in the King James that do not strike you because of your familiarity with them.

II. ANALYSIS

Segment to be analyzed: 1:1-20
Paragraph divisions: at verses 1, 4, 8, 9, 12, 17

A. Studying the Segment as a Whole

1. Lay out a work sheet on paper similar to Chart G. Note the six paragraph boxes. Use these spaces to record key words and phrases in the Bible text. (Use the margins to record your own words, such as interpretations and outlines.)

36

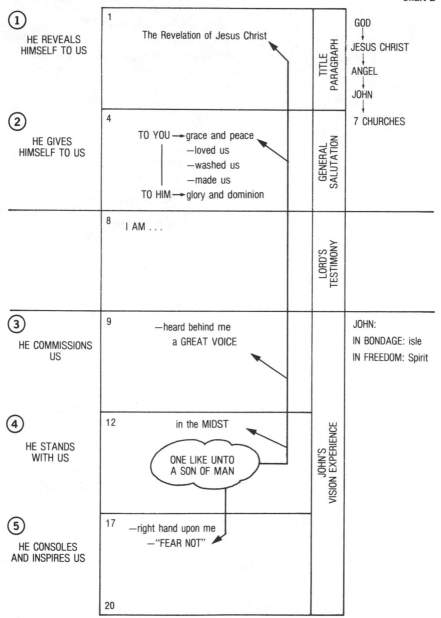

2. Read the chapter paragraph by paragraph. What is the contribution of each paragraph to this introductory chapter? Record on the work sheet.

3. Go through the chapter again, underlining strong words and phrases in your Bible. These will compose the main "materials" of your study project. Don't hesitate to mark your Bible *freely*.

4. Look at subjects common to all paragraphs. For example, what does each paragraph teach about Christ?[1] What references to *time* appear in each paragraph?

5. Study the main topical study shown on Chart G, which has these parts:

Key center: "One like unto the Son of man" (v. 13)
Master title: Jesus Christ the Son of Man
Paragraph points: He Reveals Himself to Us
                   He Gives Himself to Us
                   He Commissions Us
                   He Stands with Us
                   He Consoles and Inspires Us

Try working out a study like this on your own. Record it on your work sheet. This is a good exercise to do before looking more closely at the details of each paragraph.

B. Study of the Individual Paragraphs

Paragraph 1:1-3
1. What do the first five words tell about the theme of the entire book?

_____

_____

What is meant by "Revelation"? Read Luke 2:32, where the word "lighten," meaning "for revelation," translates the same Greek word.

_____

_____

2. Who is the original source of this "Revelation"? List the ones to whom it was given, in the correct order.

_____

_____

---

1. Some expositors interpret the speaker of 1:8 as Christ, rather than the Father (cf. 22:13). Others, however, see "Lord" (*American Standard Version,* "Lord God") as the Father.

3. Angels appear often in Revelation. For a description of their ministry, read Hebrews 1:4-14.

4. What are the references to time in this paragraph, and what do they teach? Compare 2 Peter 3:8 for God's relationship to time.

_____

_____

Paragraph 1:4-7

1. Identify these four parts in the paragraph: salutation, benediction, ascription of praise, prophetic declaration.

2. Analyze the benediction of 1:*4b*-5:

The What	To Whom	From Whom

Are all three Persons of the Trinity mentioned here? Can the one "which is, and which was, and which is to come," of verse 4, be different from the one referred to in verse 8?

_____

_____

3. Compare the benediction "Grace . . . *"unto you*,. . . and peace" (v. 4) with the ascription *"unto him* . . . be glory and dominion" (v. 6).

4. What ministries of Christ are taught here?

_____

_____

5. Note the reference to Christ's second coming in verse 7 ("he cometh"). Since He has not yet returned to the earth, what light does this throw on the time reference in 22:20, "I come quickly"?

_____

_____

Is this also a commentary on the time phrases of the first paragraph, which you observed earlier?

_____

_____

Paragraph 1:8
Note how the personal pronoun changes to "I" here, from the "he" of the previous verses. Why do you think this verse was recorded at this point? Compare 22:13.

Paragraph 1:9-11
1. How does John relate himself to his readers? To Jesus Christ?

---

2. Why was John on the isle of Patmos?

---

3. What is meant by "I was in the Spirit?"

Contrast the Patmose *bondage* and the Spirit *liberty*. Who is in control when a believer is "in the Spirit"?

---

4. Not all the churches of Asia are cited in verse 11. Does this throw light on any intended significance of *seven* churches' being listed? (See Notes on the number seven.)

Paragraph 1:12-16
1. The phrase "Son of man' (v. 13) refers to Jesus. It is His favorite title of Himself in the gospels. Read Luke 7:34 and John 5:27 for two examples. What association is represented by the title?

Try to visualize John's vision of Christ. What are your impressions?

---

2. What is taught about Christ by the symbols of the vision? To interpret each symbol, assign a spiritual application that *parallels*

the physical or material symbol. For example, white suggests purity. If there is more than one possible parallel, choose what seems to be the best one in the context.

AREA	SYMBOL	TEACHING
His person	location (v. 13): (see v. 20)	
	clothing:	
His character	head and hair (v. 14):	
	eyes:	
His activity	feet (v. 15):	
	voice:	
	hand (v. 16a):	
	mouth:	
His glory	countenance (v. 16b):	

3. Apply the interpretations of verse 20 to this vision.

_____

_____

4. How significant was it that John's first vision was one of Christ?

_____

_____

Paragraph 1:17-20
1. Account for John's reaction of verse 17*a*.

_____

_____

2. In what ways did Jesus console and inspire John? Apply this to Christians today.

_____

_____

III. NOTES

1. "Seven churches . . . seven Spirits" (1:4). The number seven, when a symbolic interpretation is intended, suggests completion, fullness. It is one of Revelation's key symbols. The seven churches represent the church as a whole; the seven Spirits represent the Holy Spirit as one Person in diverse manifestations.

2. "Washed us from our sins" (1:5). Another possible reading is "loosed us from our sins." Either reading is doctrinally correct. On the former, compare Psalm 51:2; Isaiah 1:16, 18; Acts 22:16; Ephesians 5:26; Titus 3:5. On the latter, compare Matthew 20:28; 1 Timothy 2:6; 1 Peter 1:18; Hebrews 9:12; Galatians 3:13.

3. "I was in the Spirit" (1:10). The phrase "in the Spirit" appears at four places in Revelation: 1:10; 4:2; 17:3; 21:10. Tenney builds his outline of Revelation around these points, using them as the openers of the four main visions of the book.[2]

4. "Garment down to the foot" (1:13). On the symbolism of this phrase, Vincent writes, "The long robe is the garment of dignity and honor. It may be either royal, or priestly, or both. Compare Isa. 6:1."[3]

5. "Angels of the seven churches" (1:20). The Greek word for angel means literally "messenger." We cannot be sure who the angels of the churches were. Here are various interpretations that have been made: (1) heavenly guardians; (2) human messengers; (3) rulers or teachers of the congregation; (4) a personification of the churches themselves.[4] What is your conclusion?

IV. FOR THOUGHT AND DISCUSSION

1. Is Christ *real* to you? Has your fellowship with Him ever been so intimate that you seemed to "see the voice" of Jesus (cf. 1:12)?

_____

_____

2. Why is a vision of Jesus, though not apocalyptic like John's, vital for Christian living and service?

_____

_____

3. What is the important exhortation of 1:3?

_____

_____

What should be every Christian's attitude in view of the statement "for the time is at hand" (1:3)?

_____

_____

2. Refer to Lesson 3, where this outline was shown.
3. Marvin R. Vincent, *Word Studies in the New Testament*, 2:427.
4. See ibid., pp. 433-35, for a discussion of these views.

Why has God not revealed *dates* concerning events of last times in any part of Scripture?

_____

_____

4. If you were now being severely persecuted for your Christian witness, what truths of this chapter would be an encouragement and incentive to you?

_____

_____

5. How are you impressed by the truth of the sinless Christ being "in the midst" (1:13) of local churches where sin dwells?

_____

_____

6. The seven candlesticks, symbolizing the seven churches (1:20), function as light-bearers. In what ways should the church today be such a light-bearer?

_____

_____

V. FURTHER STUDY

You may want to do further study on the following subjects, using outside helps such as doctrine books and commentaries:

1. Study references to *time* in New Testament prophecies of last things.

For example, study the Olivet Discourse of Matthew 24, which records Jesus' answer to the original question, "When?" of 24:3. Study carefully the time references in 24:32-51. Relate your study to Revelation 1:1, 3.

2. Inquire into other New Testament passages supporting the truth of Revelation 1:7 that unbelievers must eventually come face to face with Jesus.

3. In what sense has Christ made the church a "kingdom of priests" unto God (1:6)?

VI. WORDS TO PONDER

"Jesus Christ . . . the ruler of the kings of the earth" (1:5, ASV).

Lesson 5

The Seven Churches

The section of Revelation best known to Christians is chapters 2-3, the letters to the seven churches. The familiarity is mainly because of the chapters' clear content—they are mainly descriptive and do not have an abundance of difficult symbols and prophecies. They are like a mirror for the reader, as he sees himself and his church described in the letters. And who is not interested in reading about himself and his associates?

I. PREPARATION FOR STUDY

Consider for a few minutes why these two chapters are included in the book of Revelation.[1] There were, of course, the immediate spiritual needs of each of the seven churches of Asia Minor to which God wanted to address himself. Beyond that were the needs of Christians living *after* the first century. God knew when He commissioned John to write Revelation that for two or more millenniums Christians would be reading the same words of such ominous prophecies as "the time is at hand" (1:3). How could *each* generation be impressed that the book was written to *them*, as well as to their forefathers? By seeing themselves in the book. And so God chose seven churches of John's day (out of the many existing then), which were similar—individually, and as a whole—to the churches yet to be. To these seven churches John wrote the letters of chapters 2 and 3. As we study the letters we will want to see especially what they have to say about churches today, so that we can apply the truths accordingly.

---

1. Many futurists see the seven letters primarily as prophetic of successive eras of church history (see Chart C).

LETTERS TO THE SEVEN CHURCHES 2:1—3:22

Chart H

Church	Ephesus 2:1-7	Smyrna 2:8-11	Pergamos 2:12-17	Thyatira 2:18-29	Sardis 3:1-6	Philadelphia 3:7-13	Laodicea 3:14-22
Description of Christ							
Commendation							
Condemnation							
Warning							
Promise for Overcoming							
Like Churches Today							

II. ANALYSIS

Section to be analyzed: 2:1-3:22
Segment divisions: at verses 2:1, 8, 12, 18; 3:1, 7, 14

A. Study of the Section as a Whole

1. First, look at the various headings shown on Chart H. Keep these areas of study in mind as you begin reading the text.

2. Now read the passage in your Bible, underlining key words and phrases. Note such repeated phrases as "These things saith he"; "I know thy works"; "He that overcometh."

3. Read the passage a second time, recording your observations on Chart H. This is the key exercise of this lesson. Spend much time comparing the seven different messages. For example, what churches received unqualified praise? Which church is not commended for anything? How often is heaven referred to? What kinds of strong warnings appear in the letters?

B. Study of Each Letter

(Note: extend your study of each letter beyond the few selected questions given below.)
1. *To Ephesus, the orthodox but unloving church.* From Christ, the faithful companion (2:1-7).
   1. What is meant by the phrase "thou hast left thy first love" (2:4)?

_____

_____

   2. Compare the promise of 2:7 and the fulfillment in 22:2.

_____

2. *To Smyrna, materially poor but spiritually rich.* From Christ the living Saviour (2:8-11).
   1. How is *life* the keynote of this letter?

_____

_____

2. What are the enduring riches (2:9)? Relate "crown of life" (2:10) to this.

_____

_____

3. Relate 2:11 to 21:8.

_____

_____

3. *To Pergamos, tolerant of false doctrine.* From Christ the warring Lord (2:12-17).
   1. What was this church guilty of (2:14-15)?

_____

_____

Contrast this with the commendation given to the church at Ephesus, "Thou canst not bear them which are evil" (2:2).

_____

_____

How do you account for the two different words "thee" and "them" in 2:16?

_____

_____

   2. Compare the phrase "new name" (2:17) with references in 3:12; 22:4; 21:1-5.

_____

_____

4. *To Thyathira, slipping into idolatry.* From Christ the heart-searcher (2:18-29).
   1. What is the impact of the word "notwithstanding" in 2:20?

_____

   2. Compare 2:27 with 19:15.

_____

_____

   3. What is symbolized by the morning star (2:28)? (Cf. 22:16.)

_____

_____

5. *To Sardis, the lifeless church*. From Christ the coming judge (3:1-6).
   1. Study the subject of watchfulness in this letter. (Cf. Matt. 24:36-51.)

   _____

   2. Compare 3:5 and 20:12 as to the phrase "book of life." What is this book?

   _____

6. *To Philadelphia, the faithful church*. From Christ the sovereign Lord (3:7-13).
   1. What do you think is meant by "open door" (3:8)?

   _____

   2. The word "temptation" of verse 10 means trial. What does the phrase "keep thee from the hour of" mean?

   _____

   3. Write a list of the good traits and bright promises of this letter.

   _____

   _____

   4. Compare 3:12 with 21:2, 3, 22.

   _____

7. *To Laodicea, the lukewarm church*. From Christ the reigning king (3:14-22).
   1. What spiritual condition is described by the word "lukewarm" (3:16)?

   _____

   _____

2. What is the sin of verse 17? Is this a common sin today? What is Christ's solution (v. 18)?

_____

_____

3. Compare 3:21 with 22:3.

_____

_____

4. How do the verses 3:20-21 serve as a conclusion to the entire group of seven letters?

_____

_____

III. NOTES

1. "Nicolaitans" (2:6, 15). The Nicolaitans were probably a sect advocating deeds of abomination and impurity, such as heathen feasts and free love.[2]

2. "Tribulation ten days" (2:10). The reference probably symbolizes a short period of suffering.

3. "Satan's seat" (2:13). This may be a reference to an impressive altar-platform to Zeus, erected in the city of Pergamos. Or it may symbolize the city as a center of intense persecution against Christians, of which Antipas was a victim.

4. "Doctrine of Balaam" (2:14). (Cf. Num. 22-25, 31.) Of this Walvoord writes, "The doctrine of Balaam therefore was the teaching that the people of God should intermarry with the heathen and compromise in the matter of idolatrous worship."[3]

5. "That woman Jezebel" (2:20). The Jezebel of Thyatira was like the Jezebel of the Old Testament: an influential leader, corrupting her followers with immorality and idolatry (cf. 1 Kings 16:31-33; 19:2; 21:1-16; 2 Kings 9:33-35).

6. "I also will keep thee from the hour of trial" (3:10). This is not exemption from trial, but from the *hour*, or event, of trial. The pretribulation view (rapture before tribulation—see Chart E) is based partly on this verse. Walvoord comments thus:

> This passage therefore provides some support for the hope that Christ will come for His church before the time of trial and trouble described in Revelation 6 to 19. This time of tribulation will

2. Henry Alford, *The Greek Testament*, 4:563-65.
3. John F. Walvoord, *The Revelation of Jesus Christ*, p. 68.

overtake the entire world, as God inflicts His wrath upon unbelieving Gentiles as well as upon Christ-rejecting Jews.[4]

7. "I come quickly" (3:11). The intent of this expression is that Christ's coming will be sudden and unexpected, when the time arrives.

IV. FOR THOUGHT AND DISCUSSION

1. How are the seven churches of Revelation similar to churches today, in such areas as:
a. sins of the people

_____

_____

b. spiritual threats from within and from without

_____

_____

c. source of power

_____

_____

d. mission

_____

_____

2. What causes a church to be sound in doctrine but cold in practice?

_____

_____

3. What action should a church take in the problem of false teaching by members of the group?

_____

_____

4. In what sense should *overcoming* be a daily experience of the believer as well as an ultimate goal? Read what John wrote about overcoming in 1 John 5:4-5.

_____

_____

4. Ibid., p. 87.

5. Why are patience and perseverance such important Christian virtues?

_____

_____

6. What have you learned about Christ from these letters?

_____

_____

7. What do you think is the meaning behind such strong warnings as "I . . . will remove thy candlestick out of his place" (2:5); and "I will spue thee out of my mouth" (3:16)?

_____

_____

V. FURTHER STUDY

You may want to look more into the view of some futurists that 2:1-3:22 is prophetic of successive eras of church history, up to the end times. J.B. Smith's *A Revelation of Jesus Christ* is one work that may be consulted for this.[5]

VI. WORDS TO PONDER

"He that hath an ear, let him hear" (3:22).

5. J.B. Smith, *A Revelation of Jesus Christ* (Scottsdale, Pa.: Herald, 1961).

Lesson 6

Visions of God
and the Lamb

John did not see visions of fearful future judgments until his heart was first prepared and strengthened. This was accomplished through visions of glory and triumph. First came the vision of Christ the Son of Man in the midst of the churches (the vision is called a Christophany, chap. 1). Then John learned the particulars of Christ's intimate relationship to believers, from the letters to the seven churches (chaps. 2-3). Finally, the apostle in exile had visions of God on His throne (theophany) and of Christ the Lamb in the presence of that throne (chaps. 4-5). Our study of these two chapters in this lesson should reveal how John was persuaded that divine justice must triumph in the arena of human history.

I. PREPARATION FOR STUDY

1. First, refer to the survey Chart F and observe the location of 4:1–5:14 as related to the entire book. What new division begins at chapter 6?

_____

_____

2. Chart I is a survey of chapters 1-5. Refer to it in the course of your study of this lesson. Observe among other things the five songs listed.
3. Do you see injustices in the world today? Have you ever heard or asked the question, "Why do the wicked prosper, and the righteous suffer?" How mighty must be that ruler who can rise above all the principalities and powers of this world and bring judgment upon all evil? If sin must be judged, who can stand? Ponder these questions as you prepare your heart to study this lesson.

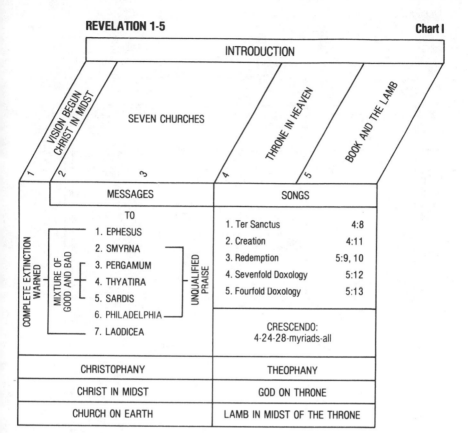

II. ANALYSIS

Segment to be analyzed: 4:1-5:14
Paragraph divisions: at verses 4:1, 6*b*, 9, 5:1, 6, 11, 13

A. Study of the Segment as a Whole

1. Make a work sheet similar to Chart J (but without the observations and outlines shown). Use this as a place to record your own observations. Each of the boxes represents a paragraph of the text.
2. Read the two chapters as one unit. What common subjects bind them together?

_____

_____

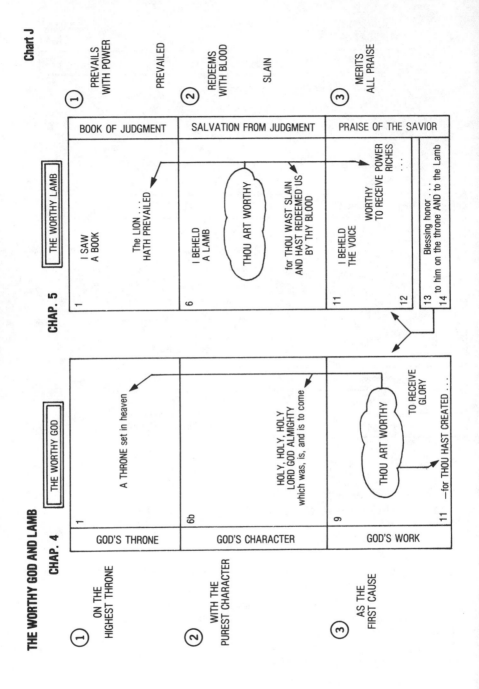

THE WORTHY GOD AND LAMB

THE WORTHY GOD

CHAP. 4

GOD'S THRONE	GOD'S CHARACTER	GOD'S WORK
1 A THRONE set in heaven	6b HOLY, HOLY, HOLY LORD GOD ALMIGHTY which was, is, and is to come	9 THOU ART WORTHY TO RECEIVE GLORY
		11 —for THOU HAST CREATED . . .

① ON THE HIGHEST THRONE

② WITH THE PUREST CHARACTER

③ AS THE FIRST CAUSE

THE WORTHY LAMB

CHAP. 5

BOOK OF JUDGMENT	SALVATION FROM JUDGMENT	PRAISE OF THE SAVIOR
1 I SAW A BOOK	6 I BEHELD A LAMB	11 I BEHELD THE VOICE
The LION . . . HATH PREVAILED	THOU ART WORTHY	WORTHY TO RECEIVE POWER RICHES . . .
	for THOU WAST SLAIN AND HAST REDEEMED US BY THY BLOOD	12
		13 Blessing honor . . .
		14 to him on the throne AND to the Lamb

① PREVAILS WITH POWER — PREVAILED

② REDEEMS WITH BLOOD — SLAIN

③ MERITS ALL PRAISE

54

3. Who is the object of worship in chapter 4? In chapter 5?

_____

_____

4. What is the main subject of each paragraph? Compare your answers with the outlines shown in the narrow vertical columns of Chart J.

_____

_____

5. Observe the statement "Thou art worthy," as it appears in 4:11 and 5:9. Make a study of this subject in both chapters.
6. Make a comparative study of the five songs of this segment. Record your observations below.

The Songs of 4:1—5:14					
PASSAGE	WHO SANG	HOW MANY SANG	ABOUT WHOM	ABOUT WHAT	SUGGESTED TITLES
4:8					"TER (three) SANCTUS (holy)"
4:10-11					
5:8-10					
5:11-12					sevenfold DOXOLOGY
5:13					fourfold DOXOLOGY

7. What are the main differences between the second and third songs?

_____

_____

8. Is there any progression in the songs? How does the last song conclude the entire group? How do you think John was impressed as he listened to the songs and to the last "Amen" of 5:14?

_____

_____

_____

B. Study of Each Paragraph

*Paragraph 4:1-6*a
1. What is the location of this setting? Compare this with the setting of chapters 1-3 and 6:1 ff.

_____

2. Who is the one sitting on the throne (cf. v. 8)?

_____

3. Of what is the rainbow symbolic (cf. Gen. 9:12-15)?

_____

4. What overall impression does this vision give?

_____

5. Try to interpret the intended meanings of each of the symbols. Who may the twenty-four elders represent? (Consider here the possibility of two groups of twelve.)

_____

_____

*Paragraph 4:6*b-8
1. Who are the main "actors" of this part of the vision?

_____

_____

What realms of creation are represented by each beast?

_____

_____

Relate this to the theme of their song (v. 8).
2. What attributes of God are referred to in the song of verse 8?

_____

_____

In what sense may these be considered *fundamental* attributes of God?

_____

3. What is the motive of the beasts' song, according to verse 9*a*?

_____

_____

Paragraph 4:9-11
1. Who sings the song of verse 11?

_____

2. Compare the two phrases: "cast their crowns before the throne" and "Thou art worthy."

_____

3. What is the key word of this song? Is the song appropriate for Christians to sing today?

_____

_____

Paragraph 5:1-5
1. What is symbolized by the words "to open the book, and to loose the seals"? For your answer, compare 6:1 ff.

_____

_____

2. What significant truth about *judgment of mankind* is taught by the words "No man . . . was able to open the book"? How is this truth emphasized in the action of this vision?

_____

_____

3. How is Christ referred to in verse 5? (Cf. Gen. 49:8-10; Isa. 11:1, 10; Matt. 22:42-45.)

_____

_____

How do these credentials qualify Him to open the book?

_____

_____

Paragraph 5:6-10
1. Compare "I saw . . . a book" (5:1) with "I beheld . . . a Lamb" (5:6).

_____

_____

_____

2. Compare the prevailing power of the Lion (5:5) with the death of the Lamb (5:6, 9).

_____

_____

What descriptions of the Lamb suggest power? In what sense is there power in the blood of Christ?

_____

_____

3. What is meant by the phrase "redeemed us to God by thy blood" (5:9)? (Cf. John 1:29; Heb. 9:12, 22; Lev. 17:14; Acts 20:28; Rom. 3:25; 5:9; 1 Pet. 1:18-19; Eph. 1:7; Col. 1:20; Rev. 1:5.)

_____

_____

In what way does the word "blood" teach that Christ's death was *sacrificial?*

_____

_____

4. Compare 5:10 and 20:6. What period of world history does this refer to?

_____

_____

Paragraph 5:11-12
The song of 5:9-10 cites the reasons that Christ is worthy to send judgment upon mankind. What aspect of Christ's worthiness is cited in the song of 5:12?

_____

_____

Paragraph 5:13-14
1. The ascription of praise (5:13) is addressed to whom?

_____

_____

2. Who sings this song? Compare Philippians 2:8-11.

_____

_____

Who says the "Amen"?

_____

_____

Who worships "him that liveth for ever and ever"? (Cf. 4:10.)

_____

_____

What does this suggest as to who the twenty-four elders may represent?

_____

_____

III. NOTES

1. "A door was opened in heaven" (4:1). One futurist view sees the church as having been raptured before the action of 4:1 begins, without actual reference to the event itself. Walvoord writes:

> The word *church,* so prominent in chapters 2 and 3, does not occur again until 22:16, though the church is undoubtedly in view as the wife of the Lamb in Revelation 19:7. She is not a participant in the scenes of the tribulation which form the major content of the book of Revelation.[1]

This is the view basically followed by this manual.

2. "Four and twenty elders" (4:4). The office of elders, who were the ruling body of their congregation, originated in Old Testament Israel (Ex. 4:29; 12:21; Num. 11:25; 1 Kings 8:1), and was carried over into the New Testament local churches (Acts 14:23; 15:6; 16:4; 20:28). The number twenty-four answers to the twelve tribes of Israel (OT) plus the twelve apostles (NT). Thus the twenty-four elders very likely symbolize the people of God of Old and New Testament times.

3. "Lightnings and thunderings and voices" (4:5). These phenomena appear before judgments fall, a pattern repeated again at 8:5; 11:19; and 16:18.

4. "Four beasts" (4:6). A more accurate translation is "four living beings" (cf. Ezek. 1:5, 19). Concerning the animals chosen for the portraits, an old rabbinical saying is this: There are four supreme orders in the world:

> among all created beings—mankins;
> among birds—the eagle;
> among domestic animals—the ox;
> among wild animals—the lion.[2]

The song of the four living creatures (4:8) and of the twenty-four elders (4:11) may be viewed as a pair. In Alford's words, "We have thus the throne of God surrounded by His Church and His

---

1. John F. Walvoord, *The Revelation of Jesus Christ*, p. 103.
2. The four animals have been likened to the four portraits of Christ in the gospels: lion, Matthew's portrait of Christ the king; calf (or ox), Mark's portrait of Christ the servant (or sacrifice); man, Luke's portrait of Christ the Son of man; eagle, John's portrait of Christ the Son of God. The similarities are very strong, though this is probably not the intended symbolism in this context.

animated world: the former represented by the 24 elders, the latter by the four living beings."[3]

5. "A book . . . sealed with seven seals" (5:1). The seals represent a series of judgments (6:1 ff). We cannot be sure of the contents of the book itself, however. Some have called it the "Book of Destiny"; others, "The Whole Counsel of God." One writer says, "The book seems to contain the story of man's losing his lordship over creation and the regaining of that authority by the Man Christ Jesus."[4]

6. "We shall reign on the earth" (5:10). This appears to be a reference to an earthly reign of saints with Christ in the Millennium, mentioned later in 20:6.

IV. FOR THOUGHT AND DISCUSSION

1. Vital questions asked by people today are like these:
   Is there a God?
   What kind of God is He, in view of the world's turmoil?
   How did the universe come into being, and what is its destiny?
   Where can I find hope for the future, especially for after death?
What answers do chapters 4 and 5 give to these questions?

_____

_____

2. Is it important for a person to know God's perspective of this world's scene? If so, why?

_____

_____

3. In what ways do these chapters teach that God the Father, Son, and Holy Spirit are alive today?

_____

_____

4. What can be learned about true worship and praise of God from this passage?

_____

_____

3. Henry Alford, _The Greek Testament_, 4:601.
4. Charles Ryrie, _Revelation_, p. 40.

Why is praise such an important part of Christian living?

_____

_____

How can worship services in our churches today be genuine, dynamic, and meaningful?

_____

_____

5. What does each item ascribed to Christ in 5:12 reveal as to who Jesus is?

_____

_____

6. If you yourself have personal assurance in Christ concerning the future, how do you feel about lost souls in the world today plunging headlong into the throes of eternal judgment?

_____

_____

V. FURTHER STUDY

1. These chapters contain the first five of Revelation's twenty songs (or hymns). Make a comparative study of all the songs of the book.

_____

_____

_____

_____

2. Compare John's vision of God with Ezekiel's (Ezek. 1:4-10, 26-28).

_____

_____

3. Study what the Bible teaches about Christ's atoning sacrifice. Answer such questions as, Why was His death necessary? and, How was His death efficacious?

VI. WORD TO PONDER

"They never stop their singing day or night: Holy, holy, holy" (4:8, TEV).

Seals of Judgment

This is the beginning of that main portion of Revelation, which foretells the world's darkest years. Chapters 6-19 are chapters of ever intensifying judgments upon man, with the hosts of darkness arrayed against God. We, like John, are assured of victory for God and Christ, even as this truth has been emphasized in the visions of chapters 1-5. The panorama of catastrophic events described in the chapters that follow (6-19) serves to show us *how* that total victory is gained. God, the Author of the book, has deemed it profitable to reveal this panorama to us, appalling as it is. Let us be wise to hear what He is saying.

I. PREPARATION FOR STUDY

1. Spend some time thinking about what may have been God's reasons to devote most of the book of Revelation to details of the end-time judgments. Your conclusions will depend in part on which of these views you hold as to the time of the church's rapture: (1) before the series of judgments; or (2) at a later time (mid- or post-tribulation).
2. What is the basic justification of divine judgment of sin, according to the Bible? One chapter to consult on this is Ezekiel 14.

3. Review your study of the last lesson, where a prominent truth was Christ's worthiness to open the seven-sealed book and so let judgment fall upon mankind. Also, keep in mind where in the book of Revelation the text of your present study is located. Chart K shows this general context.

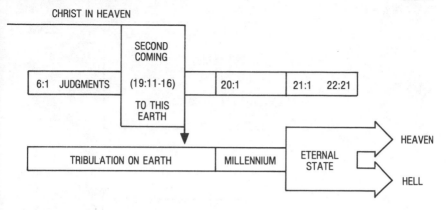

4. Be determined to complete your study of Revelation without getting bogged down in difficult places along the way. You will help yourself here by keeping in mind the study suggestions made in Lesson 2. Two key rules are: (1) proceed from the clear to the unclear; and (2) observe first; then interpret; then apply.

II. ANALYSIS

Segments to be analyzed: 6-1-17 and 7:1-17
Paragraph divisions: at verses 6:1, 3, 5, 7, 9, 12; 7:1, 9, 13

A. Observations in Chapter 6

1. Record in brief form, on Chart L, the main content of each paragraph (example is given). Assign a name to each seal.
2. What are the similarities of the first four seals?

_____

_____

How does this group of seals differ from that of the next two seals? (On the location of the seventh seal, see 8:1.)

_____

_____

3. What is the location of the action of each seal? Is there a progression in the first four seals?

_____

_____

SEALS

1   one of the seven seals   ①

—WHITE HORSE

BOW, CROWN

CONQUERING, AND TO CONQUER

3   ②

5   ③

7   ④

9   ⑤

12   ⑥

17

4. Are specific persons or groups of people identified in the first four seals?

_____

_____

How are the groups of the fifth and of the sixth seals identified?

_____

_____

5. Read Matthew 24:4-31, and note similarities between the signs prophesied by Jesus and the seals of Revelation. Keep in mind whenever you read this Olivet Discourse that Jesus' references to His future coming (e.g., 24:27, 30) are not to the rapture (His coming in the air, 1 Thess. 4:14-17) but to His coming to the earth *after* the Tribulation period (Rev. 19:11-16).

B. Interpretations of Chapter 6

1. *First seal (6:1-2)*. Some interpret the rider of the white horse to be of Satan's domain. Others take him to be Christ, the rider of the white horse of 19:11. How does the description of the next three riders favor the former view, in view of the fact that the seals are a closely knit group?
2. *Second seal (6:3-4)*. What state of the world do you see described by the words "kill one another"?
3. *Third seal (6:5-6)*. How is this a symbolic picture of famine? To answer this, apply Matthew 20:2 to the situation that a measure of wheat was approximately what a laboring man would eat in one meal.
4. *Fourth seal (6:7-8)*. The extent of death in the world is stated specifically here. Is a literal interpretation of the last sentence of verse 8 a natural one? Justify your answer.
5. *Fifth seal (6:9-11)*. In identifying these martyrs, consider the following:

a. Are these martyrs people of God?

_____

b. If the rapture of the church will take place before the seals, and if the seals are a chronological sequence, the martyrs will become believers *after* the rapture and during times of tribulation. Does the text indicate by whom they will be evangelized?

_____

_____

c. If the rapture will take place some time after the fifth seal, who are these martyrs?

_____

_____

6. *Sixth seal (6:12-17)*. What is the main characteristic of this judgment?

_____

_____

Observe the list of catastrophic signs in verses 12-14. Note that a great earthquake is cited first and appears again at the end of the list. Record the other catastrophic signs and their likenesses below:

"And the"	"As"
sun became black	sackcloth of hair

Is there any reason for not interpreting the signs of the left-hand column as actual celestial cataclysms? (Cf. Isa. 13:6-13; 34:4; Joel 2:1-2, 10, 30-31; Matt. 24:7.)

_____

_____

Is any numerical statistic of deaths cited?

_____

_____

What are the multitudes recognizing by their words of verse 17?

_____

_____

(1)

SEALED FROM
HARM ON EARTH

1

SERVANTS OF OUR GOD

(2)

PRIVILEGED TO
SING IN HEAVEN

9

(3)

QUALIFIED TO
SERVE IN HEAVEN

13

17

Does it appear from 6:17*a* that the seals are the predecessors of more severe judgments?

_____

_____

What may be the intention of the phrase "the great day of his wrath?"

_____

_____

C. Observations in Chapter 7

1. First read the chapter for main impressions. In what sense is the chapter an interlude, or parenthesis, between the six seals of chapter 6 and the trumpets beginning at chapter 8?

_____

_____

How is the question of 6:17 answered in chapter 7?

_____

_____

(Record observations on Chart M.)
2. Compare the general contents of chapters 6 and 7.

	chap. 6	chap. 7
1. earth or heaven scene (mainly)		
2. saved or unsaved (mainly)		
3. death or life		
4. place of the Lamb		
5. cry or song		

3. *Paragraph 7:1-8.* What is the purpose of the sealing?

_____

_____

What is the sealed group called in 7:3?

_____

_____

How are they specifically identified in 7:4-8?

_____

_____

Why do you think so much space is devoted to this identification?

_____

_____

Is this a clue as to whether or not this passage should be interpreted literally?

_____

_____

If this paragraph follows chapter 6 chronologically, do the 144,000 experience *seal* judgments?

_____

_____

4. *Paragraph 7:9-12.* Where is the setting of this vision?

_____

_____

Compare this with the setting of 7:1-8.

_____

_____

Who sings the song of verse 10?

_____

Compare this group with that of 7:1-8.

_____

_____

Who sings the song of verse 12?

_____

Account for the differences of theme between these two songs.

_____

_____

5. *Paragraph 7:13-17.* What does this paragraph add to the vision of 7:9-12?

_____

_____

Does this scene continue into eternity?

_____

How does this time aspect differ from the announced sequel for the 144,000 (see 7:3)?

_____

Could it be that the vision of 7:9-17 refers to a time after the entire Tribulation period is over, and not exclusively to the interim between the seals and the trumpets?[1]

_____

What resemblances to descriptions in 21:1-22:5 do you see in this paragraph?

_____

6. Does the text of chapter 7 state *how* the servants of God (7:3) and white-robed throng (7:9) are evangelized? From your study of Revelation thus far, is the *method* of evangelization discussed in any detail? If not, why not?

_____

_____

D. Interpretations of Chapter 7

1. Read Romans 11 for Paul's prophecy concerning Israel.[2] Has that prophecy been fulfilled yet?

_____

_____

1. The common phrase "After this I beheld" (7:9) does not represent sequence of fulfillment, but sequence of vision experiences.
2. That Paul means a literal nation of Israel in Romans 11 is supported by his earlier references to the Jews, such as 9:3-4; 10:1; 11:1-2.

Why is this a basis for interpreting Revelation's Israel as a literal group of Jews, in such passages as 7:4-8?[3]

_____

_____

2. According to this literal interpretation, 144,000 Jews will survive the judgment of the seals, but they must be sealed for protection from the destructive judgments that follow. What phrase in 7:1-8 identifies these Israelites as believers?

_____

_____

3. What phrases in 7:9-17 identify the "great multitude" of 7:9 as believers?

_____

_____

Would this group be different from God's "servants" of the previous paragraph? Justify your answer.

_____

_____

May the multitude include the martyrs of 6:9-11?

_____

_____

Note that 7:14 says that this multitude experienced "great tribulation." When is this tribulation?

_____

_____

If the scenes of 7:9-17 fits chronologically into the story of chapters 21 and 22, why was John given this vision at this time? (Recall the observation of survey study that songs precede judgments.)

_____

_____

3. A figurative interpretation of Rev. 7:4-8 is that "Israel" represents the true church, or all the people of God of all ages.

4. What do you think will be God's means of evangelization during the Tribulation, bringing about the salvation of Jews and non-Jews during that time?

_____

_____

III. NOTES

1. "Hell" (6:8). The Greek word is properly translated "hades," which is the unseen world of deceased unbelievers. This is how the word should be translated in the other references of Revelation, which are 1:18; 20:13, 14. The Greek word correctly translated "hell," *gehenna*, appears in such verses as Luke 12:5, but not in Revelation. In Revelation, hell is usually referred to as the "lake of fire" or "the second death" (cf. 2:11; 19:20; 20:6, 10, 14; 21:8).

2. "Fourth part of the earth" (6:8). In a world of 3 billion people, 750 million would die. Walvoord says, "Treated geographically it would be equivalent to the destruction of more than the entire population of Europe and South America."[4] Thus event the seals judgments are awesome in their dimensions.

3. "All the tribes of the children of Israel" (7:4). Although many aspects of Old Testament Israelite history typify items of the New Testament and church history,[5] the long, detailed reference to the twelve tribes in 7:4-8 suggests a literal interpretation.[6] These are believing Jews, given assurance of protection for judgments to come.

IV. FOR THOUGHT AND DISCUSSION

1. What has this passage taught you about the reasons for divine judgments upon mankind?

_____

_____

Why is it necessary to have a correct view of *who God is* to understand more fully *what He does*?

_____

_____

4. John F. Walvoord, *The Revelation of Jesus Christ*, p. 131.
5. For example, see Romans 2:28-29; Phil. 3:3.
6. See J.A. Seiss, *The Apocalypse, 1:405-6*. For the figurative view, see Martin R. Vincent, *Word Studies in the New Testament*, 2:501-2.

2. What are God's purposes in the judgments of the seals?

_____

_____

What is the effect of the sixth seal upon people?

_____

_____

What are some reasons why unbelievers today, who are informed of the gospel, refuse to be reconciled to God?

_____

_____

3. What answer is expected by the ones shouting the question, "Who shall be able to stand?" (6:17)?

_____

_____

What is a correct answer to this question as it applies to the human race?

_____

_____

4. Why is today's challenge for Christian service crucial in view of a rapture of the church before the great Tribulation?

_____

_____

How does the worldwide ministry of Christian literature today relate to this? (Cf. Matt. 24:14; 28:19-20).

_____

_____

5. How are chapters 6 and 7 a message of assurance to believers?

_____

_____

V. FURTHER STUDY

1. Various Old Testament passages prophesy the reappearance of Israel as a nation in the end times (in a "seventieth week"). Commentaries on Daniel discuss this subject. See the

author's book *Ezekiel and Daniel* for a chart showing the time of Israel's seventieth week as taught by Daniel 9:27.[7] If possible, study the entire lesson in that study manual for background to this and related portions of Revelation.

2. Consult a commentary for its elaboration on the problem passages of the list of the twelve tribes (7:4-8).

VI. WORDS TO PONDER

Two precious insights into heaven's activities are shown by the core of 7:15:

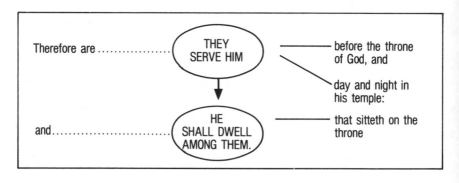

7. Irving L. Jensen, *Ezekiel and Daniel* (Chicago: Moody, 1967), p. 86.

Lesson 8

Trumpets of Judgment

The six seals of judgments have been opened, the interlude of divine sealing and saints' singing is over. John now begins to see worse judgments still, those of the trumpets. Our study of this lesson concerns the first six trumpet judgments. Recall from your survey study that the seventh trumpet (11:15) *introduces* and *is* the whole group of bowl judgments (15:5 ff.), just as the seventh seal (8:1) *introduces* and *is* the trumpet judgments.

I. PREPARATION FOR STUDY

1. The extraordinary phenomena of the trumpet judgments (as well as all the judgments that follow) defy human comprehension. Even John senses at times how inadequate the human language is in describing the visions (hence such phrases as "as it were"). It is very important for us to secure our thinking about these phenomena on a bedrock foundation. To help establish this, consider the following:

a. All the judgments have their ultimate source in God. Some are permitted by Him (e.g., 9:1); others He sends directly (e.g., 8:7).

b. The judgments are of supramundane dimensions. We should not expect God to be limited to use only what already exists. For example, the object "resembling a great mountain, blazing with fire" (8:8, *Amplified*), may be literally some immense molten mass, supernaturally made by God just for that judgment. In our interpretation we should not reject the possibility of a ful-

fillment in the realm of physical nature just because such a phenomenon has not been observed by man.[1]

c. In sending some judgments God uses the satanic world of
demons, a world which defies description. (Cf. the demonic locusts of 9:1-11). If a demon-possessed man in Jesus' day could do
suprahuman feats (Luke 8:29), what may we not expect from hosts
of demons let loose upon the world in the end times?

d. Supernatural judgments of God upon mankind are already
part of recorded history (e.g., OT history). Why should we not expect such judgments, in boundless dimensions, in the last days?
(Cf. 2 Pet. 3:1-7). For example, imagine the following to be one of
John's visions of judgment:

> And I looked, and behold, an angel cast ashes from a fiery fur-
> nace into the sky; and the sky was darkened with the dust there-
> of. And all men and beasts upon whom the dust settled were tor-
> mented with open sores; only those with the seal of God on
> their forehead escaped.

Would a literal interpretation of such a prophecy be a natural
one? If you think not, read Exodus 9:8-12 and observe that such a
plague actually fell upon the Egyptians in Old Testament days. In
this connection it would be helpful for you at this time to read the
whole series of plagues recorded in Exodus 7:14–12:36. Many of
the kinds of plagues that God sent then are similar to the ones re-
served for the end times—of smaller dimensions, but no less
miraculous.

e. The prophecies of Revelation concern two realms of fulfillment: physical, and nonphysical (e.g., spiritual, political). A *literal*
interpretation does not transfer from one realm to the other. That
is, a prophecy of a physical item will see its fulfillment in the physical world, just as a prophecy of a spiritual item will find its fulfillment in the spiritual realm. For example, a literal interpretation of
the great mountain cast into the sea (8:8) is that some large physical object (whatever it is *exactly*) will be thrust into the sea. A *figurative* interpretation, on the other hand, may see this as a power-
ful nation falling.

2. Another Old Testament passage to read in connection with
this lesson is Joel 1:1-7; 2:1-11. Read this passage again *after* you
have analyzed the two chapters of this lesson.

---

1. Even at that, this burning-mountain phenomenon is not beyond our imagina-
tion. A volcano is *part* of a mountain burning and erupting into the surrounding sea; the mountain of Revelation is a *complete* mountain so disposed of. Actually, the thing John sees in this vision is something he has never seen
before, but it resembled ("as it were") a "great mountain."

3. Study Chart N, which is a survey of the chapters 6-9. Half of the chart is a review of the last lesson; the other half gives an overview of the passage of this lesson.

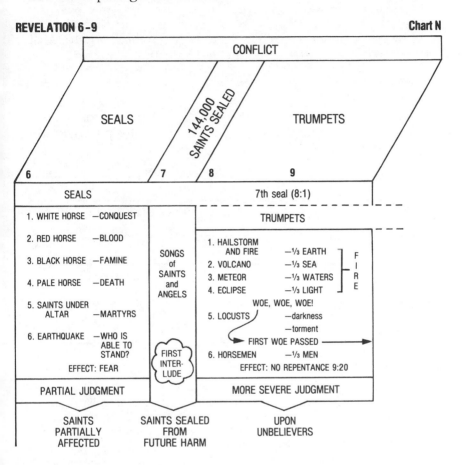

II. ANALYSIS

Segments to be analyzed: 8:1-12 and 8:13-9:21
Paragraph divisions: at verses 8:1, 3, 7, 8, 10, 12, 13; 9:1, 7, 12, 13, 17, 20

A. Segment 8:1-12

1. Read 8:1-12 for a view of the segment as a whole. Underline key words and phrases in your Bible. Observe the layout of para-

graphs on the work sheet of chart O. Mark these paragraph divisions in your Bible if you have not already done so. As you study this segment, record your observations on Chart O (words of the Bible text inside the paragraph boxes; your own words in the margins).

2. How do the first two paragraphs differ from the last four? What does each of the former contribute to the setting?

_____

_____

3. *Paragraph 8:1-2.* What is the impact of the half hour of "silence in heaven"? Contrast this with 7:9-12. What does this paragraph reveal about the source of the trumpet judgments?

_____

_____

4. *Paragraph 8:3-6.* Record the main point of each of these parts:

verses 3-4: _____

verse 5: _____

verse 6: _____

What do you think is the subject of the prayers of the saints (vv. 3-4)? Compare 6:9-11.

_____

___

Who are these saints?

_____

_____

Do you see anything of suspense in verse 6?

_____

_____

What does the blowing of trumpet notes often symbolize? Compare this with the symbol of a seal in the seal judgments.

_____

_____

1 7th seal SILENCE IN HEAVEN		SUSPENSE
3 (FIRE) cast into the earth —PREPARED THEMSELVES TO SOUND		SUSPENSE

1

7

2

8

3

10

4

12

5. Observe the word "fire" in 8:5. Scan the verses of the first four trumpets (8:7-12) and note every reference, direct or indirect, to fire. Record these on Chart O. Why is fire used in divine judgment?

_____

_____

6. *First trumpet* (8:7). Read Exodus 9:18-26 for the combination of hail and fire. What does the Exodus passage suggest as a possible interpretation of "blood" in Revelation 8:7?

_____

_____

After the word "earth" in the Bible text, this phrase (supported by the best ancient manuscripts) should be inserted: "and the third part of the earth was burnt up" (ASV). What does this reveal as to the extent of this and the other trumpet judgments, local or worldwide?

_____

_____

7. *Second trumpet* (8:8-9). What is the function of the phrase "as it were"?

_____

_____

What must we recognize when we interpret prophecies like this?

_____

_____

On the "blood" phenomenon, compare Exodus 7:17-25.
8. *Third trumpet* (8:10-11). How could one fallen star touch one-third of the world's rivers and water springs? In answering this, recall the miraculous multiplication of a handful of ashes into a cloud of dust covering the land of Egypt (Ex. 9:8-10). Also, keep in mind this modern day's phenomenon of atomic fallout.

_____

_____

What aspect of God's miracles in the Bible does He not disclose to us?

_____

_____

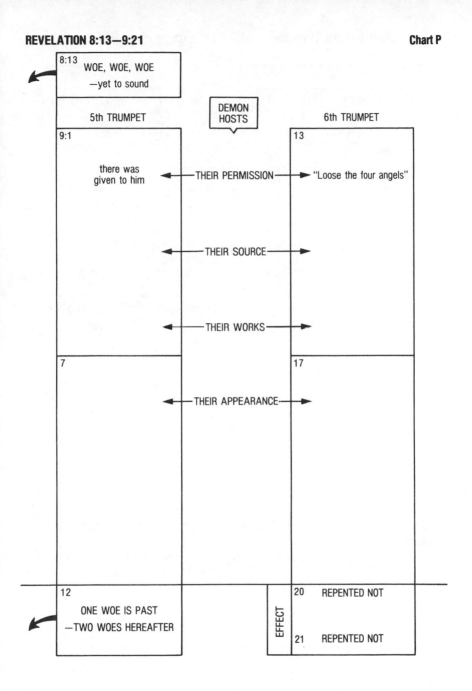

How does the third trumpet judgment affect mankind?

_____

_____

9. *Fourth trumpet* (8:12). Compare the darkness of this judgment with that of Exodus 10:21-23.

_____

_____

What brought on that darkness?

_____

_____

What will bring it on in the fourth trumpet judgment?

_____

_____

Does the word "smitten" reveal the details of God's method in bringing this judgment?

_____

_____

10. Think back over the four trumpet judgments. What do you think are God's purposes in sending them?

_____

_____

B. Segment 8:13–9:21

1. Read this segment through, as you did the previous one. Record observations on Chart P. For example, complete the outline concerning demon hosts.
2. Compare the six trumpet judgments, recording your study on Chart Q. This will help you see this series as a whole.
3. Observe that the first four judgments are inflicted directly upon nature, while the last two are upon man. Do people die as a result of any of the first four judgments?

_____

_____

Could these judgments be God's way of demonstrating to the world who is in control?

_____

_____

THE SIX TRUMPET JUDGMENTS   Chart Q

	1	2	3	4	5	6
JUDGMENT	hail, fire, blood					
IMMEDIATE OBJECT						
RESULTING DESTRUCTION						

4. What is the main difference between the fifth and sixth trumpets, concerning death of mankind?

_____

_____

5. *Paragraph 8:13.* How does the wail of this verse represent the remaining judgments of Revelation? (Cf. 9:12; 11:14; 12:12; 16:17.)

_____

_____

6. *Paragraph 9:1-6.* How does John refer to the "star" as a person in verse 1?

_____

_____

Who could this "star" be? (Cf. Is. 14:12-17; Lk. 10:18; Rev. 12:7-9.) Could the star be the "angel" of Revelation 9:11? (Note: read the word "fall," v. 1, as "fallen.")

_____

_____

Observe the repeated phrases "was given" and "was commanded." What does this teach as to who sends the judgment?

_____

_____

What is the seal of verse 4?

_____

_____

What is the purpose of this judgment?

_____

_____

7. *Paragraph 9:7-11*. What is the purpose of verses 7-10?

_____

_____

Note the frequent repetitions of "like" and "as." What label would you give to these locusts, in view of their source, appearance, leader, and work? (See Notes on v. 11.)

_____

_____

8. *Paragraph 9:13-16*. How is God shown to be the sender of this judgment?

_____

_____

From what geographical direction do the 200 million horsemen come?

_____

_____

Where is the largest nation, population-wise, located today, in relation to Bible lands?

_____

_____

Could this have anything to do with verse 14?

_____

_____

What does verse 15 teach about the appointed *time* of judgment? (Read "the hour" instead of "an hour.")

_____

_____

Does God keep all His appointments?

_____

_____

How many people are killed by this judgment? Compare this with the judgment of the fourth seal (6:4).

_____

_____

9. *Paragraph 9:17-19*. What is the main purpose of this paragraph?

_____

_____

Compare the horses and the locusts.

_____

_____

Unless the supernatural is ruled out, could these two judgments fall literally as described?

_____

_____

10. *Paragraph 9:20-21*. What is the effect of the trumpet judgments upon the survivors of the judgments thus far? Compare this with the effect of the seal judgments.

_____

_____

What two kinds of sins are listed after the two references to *no repentance*?

_____

_____

What does this paragraph teach about sinful man's love for sin?

_____

_____

Does the phrase "repented not" suggest that men under these judgments have the opportunity to repent?

11. With the help of Chart N, review your study of the six judgments of this lesson. If these prophecies are interpreted literally, is it possible that any of them have been fulfilled yet?

Answer the same question on the basis of a figurative interpretation. Be specific, as to world events, in your answer.

12. Refer to Chart L again, and fix in your mind the place of the trumpet judgments in the scheme of Revelation 6:1-22:21.

III. NOTES

1. "Altar" (8:3). The word "altar" appears eight times in Revelation: 6:9; 8:3*a*, 3*b*, 5; 9:13; 11:1; 14:18; 16:7.

2. "Saints" (8:3). A concordance shows this to be both an Old and New Testament word. The other appearances of the word in Revelation are: 8:4; 11:18; 13:7, 10; 14:12; 15:3; 16:6; 17:6; 18:24; 19:8; 20:9.

3. "An angel" (8:13). The best manuscripts read "an eagle."

4. "Bottomless pit" (9:1). Luke 8:31 translates the same Greek word (*abyssos*) as "abyss" (*Berkeley;* "deep," KJV), identifying it as the abode of demons, or wicked spirits. Satan is confined here during the millennium (Rev. 20:1-3). Other references in Revelation are: 9:2, 11; 11:7; 17:8.

5. "Locusts" (9:3). Wilbur M. Smith interprets the locusts symbolically and the horsemen (9:16) literally.[2] For the former, he cites such Old Testament verses as Deuteronomy 28:38, 42; Nahum 3:15, 17; and Amos 7:1-3 (ASV), where locusts are symbols of divine judgment.

6. "Five months" (9:5). A literal interpretation may be intended here. If symbolical, the emphasis is on the *extended* time, for *any* duration of torment is all too long.

7. "A king over them" (9:11). This phrase confirms that the locusts of this judgment are a unique host, for Proverbs 30:27 teaches that "the locusts have no king."

2. Wilbur M. Smith, "Revelation," in *The Wycliffe Bible Commentary,* p. 1509.

8. "Abaddon" (9:11). This Hebrew name means "destruction;" the Greek name Apollyon means "destroyer."

9. "Sorceries" (9:21). The evil use of drugs is intimately associated with witchcraft.[3] W.E. Vine writes:

> In sorcery, the use of drugs, whether simple or potent, was generally accompanied by incantations and appeals to occult powers, with the provision of various charms, amulets, etc., professedly designed to keep the applicant or patient from the attention and power of demons, but actually to impress the applicant with the mysterious resources and powers of the sorcerer.[4]

IV. FOR THOUGHT AND DISCUSSION

1. Think about the *dimensions* of these trumpet judgments. Do they appear catastrophic? Worldwide?

Is any time span given for the duration of any of these?[5]

Could any be accomplished in a short time?

Would we know if we were living in the days of any of these judgments?

---

2. Can the trumpet judgments from God be called restorative as well as retributive even though no one repents and turns to God as a result? Compare Romans 1:18-23, which teaches revelation of divine grace to all, even though it is rejected by most.

---

3. Our English word "pharmacy" comes from the Greek *pharmakia,* translated "sorcery."
4. W.E. Vine, *An Expository Dictionary of New Testament Words* (London: Oliphants, 19675), 4:51-52.
5. Some interpret the time reference of 9:15 to be around thirteen months, though the basis for this interpretation is weak.

3. How prevalent today are the sins mentioned in 9:20-21: materialism, Satan, worship, murder, drug addiction, immorality, theft?

_____

_____

4. What elements of God's natural world are destined for destruction?

_____

Can we be guilty today of taking for granted the beauties and blessings of nature?

_____

_____

5. What answer does the passage of this lesson give to the unbeliever who secretly counts on becoming a believer when his plight in the world becomes unbearable?

_____

_____

6. What are some very important practical lessons you have learned in your study of this lesson?

_____

_____

_____

_____

V. FURTHER STUDY

Study what the Bible teaches about the world of evil spirits. Inquire into such subjects as their origin, and their present activities. For outside reading consult Unger's *Biblical Demonology*.[6]

VI. WORDS TO PONDER

"There was utter silence in Heaven for what seemed to me half an hour" (8:1, Phillips).

6. Merrill F. Unger, *Biblical Demonology*, 5th ed. (Wheaton, Ill.: Scripture Press, 1963).

The Little Book
Two Witnesses, and
the Seventh Trumpet

We move now into the first of the parenthetical chapters which fall between the trumpet and bowl chapters. Though the sequence of seals, trumpets, and bowls is a clear progression of intensifying judgments, the visions that John saw between those of the trumpets and bowls are more difficult to interpret since they apparently do not represent a chronological sequence as such. One of the main purposes of this lesson is to show how 10:1-15:4 fits into the structure of the book of Revelation as a whole, and where its events may be located in the Tribulation period.

I. PREPARATION FOR STUDY

1. Review the parenthesis of chapter 7. Recall that the events of that chapter represent a time interval between chapters 6 and 8, anticipating what will take place in chapters 8-9.

2. Study Chart R carefully. Observe the following:

a. The locations of the two parentheses.

b. The unifying function of the seventh seal and seventh trumpet.[1]

c. The beginning of the last half of the seven-year Tribulation is associated with some of the visions of the last parenthesis. This is indicated by the content of the specific references to forty-two months (3 1/2 years) and 1,260 days (3 1/2 years) in 11:2-3. Recall the key Old Testament prophecy of Daniel 9:27, which describes a tribulation period ("one week" equals seven years) with two equal parts (3 1/2 years each).

---

1. The passage 11:14-19 is really not parenthetical, but part of the chronological movement from the trumpets to the bowls.

d. A precise beginning of the last half of the Tribulation is not shown because the order of events in the parenthesis is not strictly chronological, as will be shown later.[2] On the chart, possible locations for such a beginning do not appear earlier than chapter 10, in line with the interpretation that the six trumpets are judgments of the first half of the Tribulation.

e. The top arrows on the chart show that the action of chapter 7 anticipates events that follow; whereas 11:1–15:4 describes action before, during, or after the midpoint of the Tribulation period.[3]

f. Chapter 10, which has been called "The Author's Chapter," is set off by itself in the parenthesis section. This is because its main function is different from the other chapters, being didactic (concerning the ministry of a prophet) rather than predictive.

3. Keep this chart in mind as you study 10:1–15:4, for its reminders of context. Don't let the various complex visions of the parenthesis obscure the main pattern of the book.

THE CONTEXT OF 10:1—15:4 Chart R

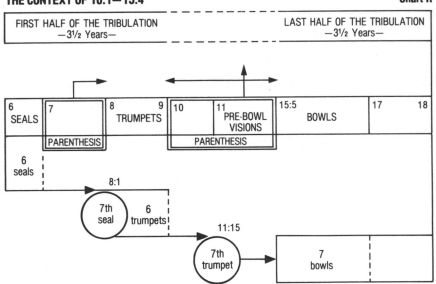

2. See John F. Walvoord, *The Revelation of Jesus Christ*, pp. 175, 186.
3. This writer sees most of the events of 11:1–15:4 as taking place during the last half of the Tribulation.

II. ANALYSIS

Segments to be analyzed: 10:1-11, 11:1-13; and 11:14-19
Paragraph divisions: at verses 10:1, 5, 8; 11:1, 3, 7, 11, 14, 19

A. Segment 10:1-11: The Little Book

1. Read the chapter for first impressions, key words, and phrases. Who is the main actor here?

_____

_____

What is the chapter's main function in the book?

_____

_____

2. Are there any prophetic utterances? If so, list them.

_____

_____

3. *Paragraph 10:1-4.* Make a list of the various symbols of this paragraph and their intended teachings. What do you think is the intent of the command "Write them not"?

_____

_____

Are some events of the end times not revealed in the Bible? If not, why not?

_____

_____

4. *Paragraph 10:5-7.* Note the triad of sea, earth, and heaven in verse 5. What is the symbolic meaning of this sight?

_____

_____

What is the angel's proclamation in verses 6 and 7? (Read "time no longer" as "no more delay.")

_____

_____

For the "seventh angel" (seventh trumpet), see 11:15. What is meant by "the mystery of God should be finished"?

_____

_____

5. *Paragraph 10:8-11.* For background to this experience of a prophet, read Jeremiah 15:16-18; Ezekiel 2:9-3:4, 14. The contents of the "little book" are not revealed. What do you think the book represents?

_____

_____

Why is such a book sweet in taste but bitter in partaking, in the life and ministry of a prophet of God?

_____

_____

Does this same truth apply to all true Christian witnesses?

_____

_____

What does verse 11 reveal about the scope and application of the book of Revelation?

_____

_____

B. Segment 11:1-13: The Two Witnesses

As you answer the questions given below, follow a literal interpretation consistently (exceptions will be pointed out), and you will sense how natural such an approach is.
1. First mark the paragraph divisions in your Bible. Then read the entire chapter. Who are the main characters in this vision? Are they identified by name?

_____

_____

2. *Paragraph 11:1-2.* What is the "holy city" (see v. 8)?

_____

_____

What specific area of the city is cited in verses 1 and 2?

_____

_____

What two groups are contrasted in these verses?

_____

_____

Could the worshipers of verse 1 be composed of Jews mainly?

_____

_____

Are the 144,000 of chapter 7 still living as of chapter 11? (Cf. 14:1, 3.)

_____

_____

What spiritual truth is suggested by the symbolic acts "measure" and "measure it not"?

_____

_____

What is the state of Jerusalem during these forty-two months?

_____

_____

3. *Paragraph 11:3-6*. Are the two witnesses persons?

_____

What is their ministry?

_____

How do the symbols of olive trees and candlesticks represent their ministry?

_____

_____

What powers are given to them? See 11:10 for the geographical dimensions of their influence.

_____

_____

Why is such power given to them at this time? Compare this power with that of the Gentiles of verse 2.

_____

_____

For how long will they minister in this manner?

_____

_____

Could this three-and-a-half-year period be the same as the one referred to in verse 2? If so, account for the angel's use of two different phrases in referring to it. (See Notes for a further discussion of this. The time element also is studied in connection with 11:14-15, below.)

_____

_____

4. *Paragraph 11:7-10.* Who would determine when the two witnesses "have finished their testimony"?

_____

_____

Compare the beast of verse 7 with the "king" of 9:11. Could these be one and the same?

_____

_____

Who shall view the dead bodies of the witnesses? Is this physically possible in today's technological world?

_____

_____

Why such worldwide rejoicing over their death?

_____

_____

5. *Paragraph 11:11-13.* How is this paragraph a commentary on the martyrdom described in the previous paragraph?

_____

_____

Is it possible that the ascension referred to in verse 12 will be viewed by the whole world?

_____

_____

What is the effect of these events on those not slain? (Note: translate "the remnant" as "the rest," referring to the survivors.)

_____

_____

Does the text of verse 13 suggest an experience of salvation or mere recognition? (Cf. Phil. 2:10-11.)

_____

_____

6. What do you think is God's purpose in the ministry of the two witnesses during the Tribulation?

_____

_____

C. Segment 11:14-19: The Seventh Trumpet

These verses pick up the movement and tone of the visions ending with the sixth trumpet of chapter 9. (In chaps. 10 and 11 John was an active participant; now he is more the beholder.)
1. Relate verse 14 to 8:13 and 9:12. If the events of 11:1-13 are placed *chronologically* between 9:12 and 11:14, then those events are to be identified with the trumpet-judgments period rather than the bowl-judgments period (see Chart R). And if that is the case, then the three-and-a-half year period of 11:2 and 11:3 would be the first half of the Tribulation, rather than the last half. If, on the other hand, 11:1-13 is considered parenthetical (the position of this manual), then its events may be placed in either half, depending on other factors.

A prominent observation that we make here is that in the section 10:1–15:4, which is generally parenthetical, we are constantly reminded (by such passages as 11:14-19) of the ongoing movement of judgments and the approaching climax of *the* final judgment.
2. *Paragraph 11:14-18.* How is the second woe of verse 14 related to the seventh angel of verse 15, in the structure of the book?

_____

_____

What is the theme of the song of verse 15?

_____

_____

Will the fulfillment be before or after the bowls?

_____

Why is the song sung at this point in John's visions?

_____

_____

For some Old Testament prophecies of this everlasting kingdom, read Daniel 2:44; Isaiah 9:6-7; Zechariah 14:9. Make a list of all the truths taught in the song of the twenty-four elders (11:17-18).

_____

_____

3. *Paragraph 11:19.* Where is this temple located, according to the text?

_____

_____

Compare this with the temple of verse 1. Also, account for the absence of a temple, according to 21:22.

_____

_____

What is the significance of the appearance of "the ark of his covenant" (ASV; "testament," KJV), at this point?

_____

_____

How do the natural phenomena of verse 19*b* introduce further judgments?

_____

_____

4. There is no intended progression in the various references of the parenthetical section to the three-and-a-half-year period of the great Tribulation. Therefore it would help you to record these references on a chart, as they appear in the text, identifying them either with the first or the last half of the Tribulation. Commentaries may be consulted for help in this. This manual will make suggestions also. Let your decisions be open to change as you proceed in

your study of the book. Place the following on Chart S: Seals and trumpets (chaps. 6-9); bowls (chaps. 15-16); first and second woes (8:13–11:14); third woe and seven trumpet (11:14-15); Jerusalem trodden (11:2); two witnesses prophesying (11:3). Keep adding to the chart as you study later passages.

THE TWO HALVES OF THE GREAT TRIBULATION   **Chart S**

THE GREAT TRIBULATION	
3½ years (Dan. 9:27) 3½ years	

III. NOTES

1. "Measure" (11:1). "The measuring itself seems to be an act of knowing, claiming or staking out. In this act of John, God is giving assurance that He will take note of those who faithfully worship Him in the Tribulation days."[4]

2. "Forty and two months" (11:2). Expositors who interpret this (and the 1,260 days of 11:3) literally, differ as to whether the three-and-a-half-year period is the first half of the Tribulation, or the last half.[5] You may want to postpone making your own decision on this until after you have studied the chapters that follow.

---

4. C.C. Ryrie, *Revelation*, p. 71.
5. For example, here are the views of three premillennial scholars: Charles Ryrie interprets the 42 months of 11:2 as the last half of the Tribulation, and the 1,260 days of 11:3 as the first half; John Walvoord interprets both as the last half; Wilbur Smith sees both as the first half. Consult their commentaries for the reasons behind these interpretations.

3. "Two witnesses" (11:3). There is no clear clue as to who these witnesses will be. Some have suggested such Old Testament resurrected heroes as Moses and Elijah. Walvoord says, "It seems far preferable to regard these two witnesses as two prophets who will be raised up from among those who turn to Christ in the time following the rapture."[6]

4. "Beast . . . out of the bottomless pit" (11:7). The beast is Satan. The word "beast" occurs frequently in Revelation. Eighteen times (e.g., 4:6) in the King James Version it translates the word *zoon*, "living creature." Thirty-five times (e.g., 11:7) it translates *therion*, "wild beast."

5. "Ark of his testament [covenant]" (11:9). "This may be a symbol of God's carrying through His covenant of grace to the end."[7]

IV. FOR THOUGHT AND DISCUSSION

1. What are various "bitter" aspects of being a true witness of Jesus Christ in today's world?

_____

_____

How important is it then to taste continually of the sweet Word?

_____

_____

2. If you are studying in a group, share your views on where the time references of 11:2-3 belong. Such a discussion will help to clarify in your mind the other clearer parts of the prophetic timetable.

3. What main spiritual lessons can be learned from the story of the two witnesses?

_____

_____

4. What attitude should the Bible student have concerning a text whose meaning is obscure?

_____

_____

6. Walvoord, p. 179.
7. Footnote in *Berkeley Version*.

V. FURTHER STUDY

Investigate the view that the rapture of the church takes place at 11:12 with the words "Come up hither." For this view, consult Norman B. Harrison, *The End.*

VI. WORDS TO PONDER

"The mystery of God will reach completion in agreement with the good news. He gave His servants the prophets" (10:7, *Berkeley*).

The Woman, Dragon, and Two Beasts

This is the concluding part of the parenthetical section between visions of the trumpets and bowls. The prophetic section of Revelation (chaps. 6-22) records key events of the last days mainly as they affect the whole world living at that time. Some small parts of the book are devoted to the special subject of the destiny of Israel.[1] Because the descriptions of the seals, trumpets, and bowls are universal in character, without singling out Israel as such, some of the chapters in the parenthetical section supplement those visions by describing key events of Israel during that Tribulation period.[2] This may be seen from this listing:

Chap. 10: A personal chapter concerning John
Chap. 11: Jerusalem and its inhabitants; the Temple (two witnesses—Jews?)
Chap. 12: Dragon vs. the Woman (Israel)
Chap. 13: Are the saints of verse 7 mainly Jewish believers?
Chap. 14: 144,000 of Israel (v. 1); most of the chapter looks forward to the final judgment.

I. PREPARATION FOR STUDY

1. Read Daniel 7 for background to John's visions of the beasts (chap. 13).

1. Those who do not see Old Testament prophecies of Israel as referring to the end times interpret Revelation's references to Israel as figurative of the church. Romans 11 and Palestinian current events are two of the strongest evidences that Israel as a nation has a part in the history of the end times.
2. This is why the parenthetical section is not a chronological progression from the trumpets to the bowls. Depending on the particular subject of a vision in that section, the passage may refer *back* to, say, the trumpets, or *forward* to the bowls.

REVELATION 10-22

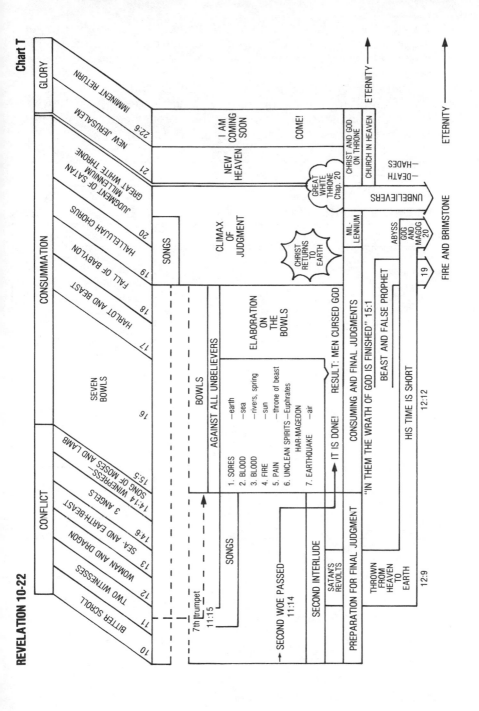

GLORY

IMMINENT RETURN

NEW JERUSALEM 22:6

CONSUMMATION

NEW JERUSALEM / MILLENNIUM GREAT WHITE THRONE 21

JUDGMENT OF SATAN 20

HALLELUJAH CHORUS

FALL OF BABYLON 19

HARLOT AND BEAST 18

17

16 SEVEN BOWLS

15:5 SONG OF MOSES AND LAMB

14:14 WINEPRESS—

14:6 3 ANGELS

SEA- AND EARTH-BEAST

13 WOMAN AND DRAGON

12 TWO WITNESSES

11 BITTER SCROLL

10

CONFLICT

I AM COMING SOON

COME!

NEW HEAVEN

CLIMAX OF JUDGMENT

CHRIST RETURNS TO EARTH

CHRIST AND GOD ON THRONE

CHURCH IN HEAVEN

—DEATH—
—HADES—

GREAT WHITE THRONE Chap. 20

UNBELIEVERS

MIL-LENNIUM

ABYSS

GOG AND MAGOG 20

19

FIRE AND BRIMSTONE

ETERNITY ——

ETERNITY

SONGS

ELABORATION ON THE BOWLS

BOWLS

AGAINST ALL UNBELIEVERS

1. SORES —earth
2. BLOOD —sea
3. BLOOD —rivers, spring
4. FIRE —sun
5. PAIN —throne of beast
6. UNCLEAN SPIRITS—Euphrates
   HAR-MAGEDON
7. EARTHQUAKE —air

IT IS DONE!

RESULT: MEN CURSED GOD

"IN THEM THE WRATH OF GOD IS FINISHED" 15:1

CONSUMING AND FINAL JUDGMENTS

BEAST AND FALSE PROPHET

HIS TIME IS SHORT

12:12

SONGS

7th trumpet
11:15

SECOND WOE PASSED
11:14

SECOND INTERLUDE

SATAN'S REVOLTS

PREPARATION FOR FINAL JUDGMENT

THROWN FROM HEAVEN TO EARTH

12:9

103

2. Chart T is an expanded survey of chapters 10-22. Study it to get the feel of the surrounding context of the three chapters of this lesson. Observe, for example, the disposition of Satan from the time of chapter 12 to that of chapter 20.

3. Scan chapters 12-14 for their highlights, and record these in brief form in the paragraph boxes of Chart U (examples shown). (Mark the paragraph divisions in your Bible before you read.) How is chapter 14 different from chapters 12 and 13?

HIGHLIGHTS OF CHAPTERS 12-14   Chart U

Chap. 12	Chap. 13	Chap. 14
1 —a woman —red dragon —man-child —woman fled	1	1
7	5	6
13	11	12
		14
17	18	20

II. ANALYSIS

Segments to be analyzed: 12:1-17; 13:1-18; 14:1-20
Paragraph divisions: at verses 12:1, 7, 13; 13:1, 5, 9, 11; 14:1, 6, 12, 14

A. Segment 12:1-17

1. Who are the main characters of each of the three paragraphs?

_____

_____

2. *Paragraph 12:1-6.* Who is the red dragon, according to verse 9?

_____

Since the text itself interprets this phrase figuratively, we have strong support to interpret other parts of the sign in like manner when this seems more adequate than a literal interpretation. For example, who do you think the man-child and the woman are?

_____

_____

Read Isaiah 26:17-18; 66:7 ff.; Micah 4:10; 5:3 in connection with the interpretation that the woman is Israel and the man-child is Jesus. In what sense did Israel bring forth Jesus?

_____

_____

Did Satan attempt to kill Jesus when He was born (cf. Matt. 2:16-18)?

_____

_____

How is Genesis 3:15 (known as the "protevangelium," or first evangel) related to this paragraph?

_____

_____

When was Jesus "caught up unto God" (v. 5)?

_____

_____

If the 1,260 days of verse 6 represent a part of the Tribulation, how long an interval is there between verse 5 and verse 6?

_____

_____

Record on Chart S which half of the Tribulation you think is meant by verse 6. (See Notes.)

3. *Paragraph 12:7-12*. What is meant by "war in heaven" (v. 7)?

_____

_____

In what sense does Satan have access to heaven today? (Cf. Job 1:12.)

_____

_____

According to verses 9 and 10, Satan will be cast out of heaven to the earth. When will this be, according to verses 13 and 14? (Note: the phrase "a time, and times, and half a time" is another way of saying three-and-a-half-years, the units being 1 + 2 + 1/2.)

_____

_____

Does the casting down of Satan to the earth (12:9) occur before his pursuit of the woman and the three-and-a-half-year period? (Cf. Rev. 12:7 and Dan. 12:1.)

_____

_____

Does it appear then that Satan is cast down at the beginning of the last half of the Tribulation? Record this on Chart S.
How is Satan described in verse 9?

_____

_____

Why is his being cast down to the earth such a woeful event (v. 12)?

_____

_____

4. *Paragraph 12:13-17*. Note how often the word "woman" appears here. Observe that the birth of the man-child and the woman's flight to the wilderness, first recorded in 12:5-6, are recorded again in verses 13 and 14. Thus this paragraph gives an expanded description of the persecution mentioned in the former verses. Follow the interpretation suggested earlier that this woman represents Israel.
How do you interpret the "wilderness"?

_____

_____

If "water as a flood" (v. 15) is not taken literally, how does the symbolism of Isaiah 59:19 suggest an interpretation?

_____

_____

How does the word "war" of Revelation 12:17 support the symbolical view?

_____

_____

Is Israel protected during this period?

_____

_____

Verse 17 suggests that when Satan cannot slay Israel as a nation, he makes war with the rest of her offspring, composed of believers who apparently did not flee with the other Jews.[3] Verse 17 is unclear as to the action prophesied because no further details are given.

B. Segment 13:1-18

Observations

Read the chapter once or twice, marking key words and phrases in your Bible. Then answer the following questions, citing the verses that supply the answers.

1. Who are the two main "actors" of this chapter?

_____

2. Is the sea beast of verse 1 different from the dragon?

_____

3. List these in the order of their authority or position: sea beast, dragon, and earth beast (v. 11).

_____

_____

---

3. The KJV translates this word as "remnant," though, as C.C. Ryrie points out, the Greek word *loipoi*, as it appears in Revelation, "applies to groups of individuals in a general sense and not necessarily a spiritual remnant" *(Revelation*, p. 81). Of course, as v. 17b clearly states, the people of this *loipoi* are believers.

4. What various kinds of false worship are mentioned in the chapter?

_____

_____

5. What are the two different kinds of evil activity of the sea beast?

_____

_____

6. For how long does the sea beast exercise the supramundane power given him? Record this on Chart S.
7. What powers does the earth beast exercise?

_____

_____

8. Whom does the earth beast exalt? (Note: the "first beast," or sea beast, of 13:12 is the same as the one referred to only as "the beast" in the remainder of the paragraph.")

_____

_____

9. What part of everyday life will be affected by the mark of the beast?

_____

_____

10. Are verses 9 and 10 part of a vision? Why do you think the verses appear here?

_____

_____

Interpretations

Now let us arrive at interpretations concerning at least the main items of this chapter. (The fact that some interpretations are suggested by the manual should not discourage you from formulating your own conclusions.)
1. The sea beast is generally taken to represent a secular world power, whereas the earth beast is seen as a religious world power.[4] Answer the questions that follow on the basis of this interpretation.

4. For example, see 17:12, which indicates that the ten horns of 13:1 represent ten kings (cf. Dan. 7:7).

2. What does 13:2 teach about Satan's power? Recall 12:12.

_____

_____

3. According to 13:7, saints are the object of the sea beast's attacks. Who could these saints be?

_____

_____

4. Read 15:2, keeping in mind that chapter 15 introduces the bowls of chapter 16. Are the beast's slayings of chapter 13 *before* the bowl judgments? (Cf. also 16:2.)

_____

_____

5. Concerning 13:8, make these comparative studies: relate the word "life" to "slain," and the phrase "Lamb slain" (13:8) to the phrase "overcome them" (13:7).

_____

_____

Why is the death of Christ the key to the solution of the world's problems of whatever era?

_____

_____

6. Why would a religious power (earth beast) be so interested in a secular power (sea beast)?

_____

_____

Do you see anything of such a relationship in the world today?

_____

_____

Do you think the beasts of chapter 13 represent individual persons, groups, or ideologies?

_____

_____

7. What is the intent of the phrase "It is the number of a man" (13:18)?[5]

_____

_____

If the number seven is the number of perfection and wholeness, what does the number 666 suggest?

_____

_____

8. Concerning the earth beast of 13:11, read 16:13; 19:20; 20:10. The false prophet is very likely the earth beast. If this identity is correct, project the action of chapter 13 into later chapters, using Chart T.

C. Segment 14:1-20

1. First, read the chapter through for an overview of its contents. What are your first impressions after coming from chapter 13?

_____

_____

How is this chapter an appropriate conclusion to the section 12:1–14:20?

_____

_____

2. The climax of judgment in the book of Revelation begins at chapter 15. Thus chapter 14 prepares the way for that climax by describing different visions of John about the two ultimate destinies: triumph of the righteous and judgment of the evil world. Scan the chapter again to see how these two subjects appear.
3. In your study of the chapter do not attempt to find a chronological pattern, for the approach of the visions is topical. Since there is *order* in this topical approach (e.g., note the sequence of angels in vv. 6-20), see if you can detect any topical pattern in the order of the paragraphs. (A work sheet of an analytical chart will be of much help in such a study.)

_____

5. A possible translation of this statement is: "It is the number of man." (See Leon Morris, *The Revelation of St. John,* p. 174.)

4. *Paragraph 14:1-5*. What is taught here about the preservation of the 144,000 who had been sealed for that very purpose (chap. 7)?

_____

_____

In what sense are these saints "firstfruits unto God and to the Lamb" (14:4)?

_____

_____

Could the action of this paragraph be located, timewise, toward the end of the book of Revelation?

_____

_____

5. *Paragraph 14:6-11*. From the time references of this paragraph, does the action take place before or after the last of world history?

_____

_____

Does it appear that there is opportunity for salvation even in the darkest tribulation?

_____

_____

Does this coincide with your earlier studies made in Revelation?

_____

_____

How are verses 9-11 related to chapter 13?

_____

_____

On the reference of verse 8 to Babylon, see 16:19; 17:5; 18:2, 10, 21; (this subject will be studied later). What is the main point of this paragraph?

_____

_____

6. *Paragraph 14:12-13*. What is the instructive purpose of this short paragraph located between its surrounding paragraphs?

_____

_____

Compare this with 13:9-10.

_____

_____

7. *Paragraph 14:14-20*. What is the main point of this paragraph?

_____

_____

Observe the two harvests: the reaping of 14:15-16 and the gathering of 14:17-20. Some interpret that the ones judged are the same in both cases, and are unbelievers. Others interpret the first judgment to be of believers; the second, of unbelievers. What do you think?

_____

_____

What does verse 20 teach?

_____

_____

Where would you place this paragraph, timewise, in the chronology of Revelation?

_____

_____

8. For a concluding exercise in 12:1–14:20, make a list of all that is taught in the passage about Christ and about God.

_____

_____

_____

It is interesting to note that the Lamb appears in each of the three chapters. Why is the message of the slain Lamb so important in the book?

_____

_____

III. NOTES

1. "Rod of iron" (12:5). Psalm 2:9 uses this phrase in its messianic prophecy.

2. "1,260 days" (12:6). Walvoord sees this as the last half of Daniel's seventieth week (Dan. 9:27), because "Israel is in comparative tranquillity and safety" in the first half of that week.[6]

3. "War in heaven" (12:7). For other passages on a similar theme, see 1 Kings 22; Job 1, 2; Zechariah 3; Luke 10:18.

4. "Michael" (12:7). Michael the archangel (cf. Jude 9) is the traditional champion of Israel (Dan. 10:13; 12:1).

5. "Satan" (12:9). Satan's character is revealed by his name (*Satan* means "adversary") and by his various titles: "dragon" suggests fierceness; "serpent" suggests deceit; "devil" means accuser or slanderer.

6. "Beast . . . out of the sea" (13:1). Ryrie identifies this beast as the antichrist of 1 John 2:18. He writes:

> The title "antichrist" . . . ought to be applied to the outstanding person among all these false people, and that is the first beast. Also . . . the first beast (whether you call him antichrist or not) is the man of sin (2 Thess. 2:3), the little horn (Dan. 7:8), the prince that shall come (Dan. 9:26), the willful king (Dan. 11:36), and the beast (Rev. 11:7; 14:9, 11; 15:2; 16:2, 10, 13; 17:3-17; 19:19-20; 20:4, 10).[7]

7. "666" (13:18). One writer has remarked that this famous number has been made to yield almost all the historical names of the past eighteen centuries. A sound interpretation is to see the number as an emphatic form of six, which symbolically is the number of fallen man. How literally the prophecy will be fulfilled, as to the number itself, is difficult to say.

8. "Firstfruits" (14:4). On the word "firstfruits," compare James 1:18. Ryrie sees the 144,000 as firstfruits of many other Israelites "who will turn to the Lord at the end of the tribulation and during the millennium (Isa. 2:3; Zech. 8:22)."[8]

9. "Here is the patience . . ." (14:12). *Today's English Version* reads: "This calls for endurance on the part of God's people."

10. "Blood . . . out of the winepress, even unto the horse bridles" (14:20). Because of the details, some interpret this description of bloodshed literally. This writer prefers the figurative view

6. John F. Walvoord, *The Revelation of Jesus Christ,* p. 191.
7. Ryrie, p. 87.
8. Ibid., p. 89

that here is a picture of bloodshed so profuse that only amplified dimensions can adequately represent the carnage.

IV. FOR THOUGHT AND DISCUSSION

1. Discuss the past history of Israel, from the time of the birth of the nation (Gen. 12) to the present.

_____

_____

_____

How do you account for the preservation of this nation despite severe persecutions and judgments?

_____

How do you explain the miracle of the rebirth of Israel as a nation on May 14, 1948?

_____

2. From the divine standpoint, why is so much tribulation in store for Israel in the last days?

_____

What enemies are lined up against Israel today?

_____

How precarious is the Middle-East situation?

_____

3. How do you account for miracles by satanic powers, such as those of chapter 13?

_____

_____

4. Why do people blaspheme God?

_____

5. How real is the eternal punishment of "fire and brimstone" referred to in 14:10-11?

_____

6. Discuss the "wrath of God, which is poured out without mixture into the cup of his indignation" (14:10).

_____

7. What are the prominent spiritual lessons of chapters 12-14?

_____

_____

_____

_____

V. FURTHER STUDY

1. Study the names and titles of Satan in Scripture.
2. With the help of books on the subject, study what the Bible teaches about the Antichrist of the last days.
3. You may want to make an extended study of the topic "The wrath of God" as this appears under different words in the Bible. Use outside helps such as *Nave's Topical Bible* and W.E. Vine's *An Expository Dictionary of New Testament Words.*[9]

VI. WORDS TO PONDER

"They are without fault before the throne of God" (14:5).

---

9. O.J. Nave, *Nave's Topical Bible* (Chicago: Moody, 1921); and W.E. Vine, *An Expository Dictionary of New Testament Words* (London: Oliphants, 1965).

Lesson 11

Bowls of Judgment

The last series of judgments upon the world—the seven bowls—is the subject of this lesson. We have been studying the progression of judgment in the earlier series of the seals and trumpets, and have noted various indications that the worst is yet to come. The bowls constitute the third and most awful of the three woes that were announced to the inhabitants of the earth just before the fifth trumpet (8:13). And when the last of the bowls is poured, heaven's pronouncement is terse yet triumphant: "It is done" (16:17).

I. PREPARATION FOR STUDY

1. Review Chart T for a survey of the context of our present passage.
2. Recall that the effect of the seal and trumpet judgments upon mankind was that men hardened their hearts more and more against the very thought of God. (See Chart N.) What have you learned about the long-suffering of God in your study of Revelation thus far?

_____

_____

3. Keep in mind that the bowl judgments do not cover the entire last half of the great Tribulation. Recall that the sea beast's slayings of chapter 13 take place during this last three-and-a-half-years but *before* the bowl judgments, as indicated by 15:2.

II. ANALYSIS

Segments to be analyzed: 15:1-8; 16:1-21
Paragraph divisions: at verses 15:1, 2, 5; 16:1, 8, 12, 17

A. Prelude to the Bowl Judgments (15:1-8)

As you read the chapter, try to visualize the sights and hear the sounds. How does this chapter introduce the bowls?
1. Seven angels (15:1).
    1. How is this sign described?

    _____

    _____

    2. What words reveal the *finality* of the bowl judgments?

    _____

    _____

2. Songs (15:2-4).
    1. Observe the two references to song (v. 3). On the song of Moses, compare Exodus 15 and Deuteronomy 32. How might the lines of verses 3-4 be seen as the song of the Lamb? Consider the possibility that the song of the Lamb is Psalm 22.

    _____

    _____

    2. Who are the singers? When had they been martyred?

    _____

    _____

    3. Analyze the song itself. Complete the following outline:
        THY WORKS:
        THY WAYS:
        THY SELF:
    4. Recall from your survey study that songs precede judgments in the book of Revelation.
3. The temple opened (15:5-8).
    1. Why does the temple (literally "sanctuary," which was the inner holy place of the Tabernacle) play such an important part in the setting of the beginning of the bowl judgments?

    _____

    _____

    2. How does the scene of verse 8 introduce the bowls? What two attributes of God are cited in verse 8?

    _____

    _____

On the phenomenon of smoke, compare Exodus 19:18; 40:34-35; Isaiah 6:4.

B. The Seven Bowls (16:1-21)

1. After you have read the chapter as a unit, compare the seven bowls by recording your observations on Chart V.

THE SEVEN BOWLS Chart V

	1	2	3	4	5	6	7
JUDGMENT							
IMMEDIATE OBJECT							
RESULTING DESTRUCTION							
EFFECT ON MEN'S HEARTS							

2. Compare the first six bowls with the first six trumpets (Lesson 8). Observe, for example, the similar sequence in the first four judgments, involving (1) earth, (2) sea, (3) waters, (4) sun. Can you think of a reason for such similarity between two *different* series of judgments?

_____

_____

3. Observe how often the word "great" appears in this chapter.[1] In what different ways are the bowl judgments the most severe of the three series?

_____

_____

_____

---

1. The vividness of John's apocalyptic visions is suggested by the fact that the word "great" appears seventy-two times in the book.

4. *First bowl* (16:2). Compare the judgment with the price paid for it (13:17).

_____

_____

Second bowl (16:3). Read "every living soul" as "every living creature."
Third bowl (16:4-7). Why is this bowl worse than the second?

_____

_____

In the ascription of verses 5-6, compare these phrases:

    Thou are righteous ⟶ thou hast _____

    They are worthy   ⟶ they have _____

Fourth bowl (16:8-9). Compare the two effects: men blasphemed, and repented not.

_____

_____

Fifth bowl (16:10-11). Why does God bring the throne of the sea beast into one of His judgments? Who are the "they" of verse 10?

_____

_____

Sixth bowl (16:12-16). List the main parts of this judgment.

_____

_____

_____

Why the parenthetical statements of verse 15?

_____

_____

What earlier judgments also involved movement of forces from the east (e.g., Euphrates)?

_____

_____

Is it possible that the invasion of the army of the sixth trumpet (9:15) is an early stage of judgment that comes to full scale at a later time in the sixth bowl?

_____

_____

Note the reference to Satan, the earth beast, and the sea beast, respectively, in verse 13.[2] What is the scope of the battle of verse 14? Where will it be fought? (See Notes.)

_____

_____

Locate the Plain of Megiddo on the map of Palestine. Although the action of the battle centers about this geographical location, the extent of the battle would be far-reaching (E.g., note the 200 miles of 14:20.) Chart W shows the time of this battle, in the premillennial timetable.

THE WORLD'S LAST TWO BATTLES   **Chart W**

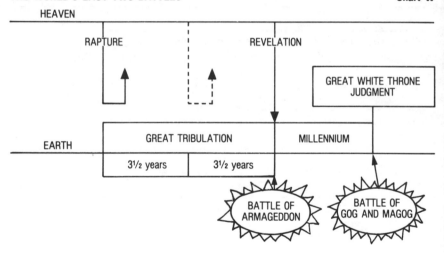

2. This threesome is sometimes referred to as the "counterfeit trinity."

Seventh bowl (16:17-21). List the main parts of this judgment: cataclysms in nature:

_____

_____

destruction in government:

_____

_____

plague upon men:

_____

_____

How thorough and devastating is the cataclysm of verse 20?

_____

_____

Concerning Babylon, recall the first reference to this city in 14:8. The next lesson (chaps. 17-18) treats this subject in detail.

_____

_____

What is the last notation of this last bowl judgment?

_____

_____

III. NOTES

1. "King of saints" (15:3). The word "saints" should read "nations."

2. "Vials" (15:7). The word is usually translated "bowls."

3. "No man was able to enter into the temple, till . . . " (15:8). John Albert Bengel comments on this:

> When God pours out His fury it is fitting that even those who stand well with Him should withdraw for a little, standing back in profound reverence till by and by the sky becomes clear again.[3]

3. Quoted by Wilbur M. Smith, "Revelation," in *The Wycliffe Bible Commentary*, p. 1514.

4. "Armageddon" (16:16). The Hebrew is Har Meghiddo ("Hill of Megiddo") which overlooks the vast plain area located southwest of the Sea of Galilee. Many battles in the Old Testament were fought here (e.g., Judg. 4, 7).

5. "Weight of a talent" (16:21). In John's day a talent weighed around one hundred pounds.

IV. FOR THOUGHT AND DISCUSSION

1. On the basis of what the book of Revelation records up to chapter 15, what will be the state of the world just before the bowl judgments are meted out? Consider these realms: the physical world of nature; people's hearts, minds, and bodies; and local and world government.

_____

_____

_____

2. What impresses you about the fact of *many* partial judgments falling upon man before *the* final great white throne judgment of chapter 20? What are God's purposes in such an extension?

_____

_____

_____

V. FURTHER STUDY

If you have not already done so, study the various songs of Revelation for what they teach about God's attributes. Begin with the song of 15:3-4.

VI. WORDS TO PONDER

"Listen! I am coming like a thief! Happy is he who stays awake" (16:15, *Today's English Version*).

Lesson 12 *Revelation 17:1–18:24*

The Fall of Babylon

The power and wealth of men and nations of the world will reach a peak toward the close of history. This is foretold in the visions of chapters 17 and 18. At that very peak will come the awesome collapse of a city and a system, "Babylon the great is fallen!" (18:2), a sign to the world that the final consuming fires of divine judgment are at hand.

In your study of this passage you will observe that the vision not only foretells Babylon's fall, but it also says much about Babylon's sins. As you think back over the chapters of Revelation that you have studied, you may recall that there is no *extended* description of the sins of the unbelieving world in those chapters. Hence the prominence of this subject in the passage of the present lesson. It is interesting to observe in this connection that this passage about Babylon constitutes almost 14 percent of the prophetic chapters 6-22.

Actually the subject of Babylon is not new to us at this point in our study of Revelation. Recall that at 14:8 and 16:19 the fall of the "great city" was associated with God's "hour of . . . judgment" (14:7) and with the end of His bowl judgments ("It is done," 16:17). Now, with all the bowl judgments recorded, it is the appropriate time for John to backtrack and describe in detail his vision of fallen Babylon.

I. PREPARATION FOR STUDY

1. In your study of these two chapters you will want to know how to interpret "Babylon." For background to this study, read Genesis 10:10 and 11:1-9, which are the earliest Bible references to the city ("Babel," meaning "gate of God," is the Hebrew form of "Babylon"). Locate the city of Babylon on a map. Also consult an exhaustive concordance and note how often the name "Baby-

lon" appears in Old Testament history. If you are acquainted with that history, recall the important relations of the Babylonian empires to the kingdom of Israel. Finally, read an article on Babylon in a Bible dictionary, which should impress you with the fact of the city's splendor before its fall, in the centuries before Christ. For many generations the name Babylon was a symbol of greatness to the world at large.

2. Observe on Chart T the context of chapters 17 and 18. The chart identifies this section as an elaboration on the bowls. The fall of Babylon is not a new event of judgment, but is associated with the bowl judgments. Note how the first phrase of 17:1 is related to chapter 16. Review chapter 16, keeping the bowl judgments in mind as you study this lesson.

II. ANALYSIS

Segments to be analyzed: 17:1-18 and 18:1-24
Paragraph divisions: at verses 17:1, 3, 6*b*, 15; 18:1, 4, 9, 11, 17, 21

1. After you have marked the paragraph divisions in your Bible, read the two chapters in one sitting, for general impressions. Are both chapters about the same general subject?

_____

_____

2. Who is the main person of chapter 17?

_____

_____

Do you agree that the "great city" Babylon is the main subject of chapter 18?

_____

_____

What specific evidences in chapter 17 clearly identify the woman as being that great city?

_____

_____

Are these Bible texts making a literal or figurative interpretation of the meaning of "woman"?

_____

_____

3. Clearly, then, the woman represents Babylon (17:18). Our next question is, What is Babylon? There are four possible answers:

a. Babylon is a real city, located on the original site of Babylon (on the Euphrates River).

b. Babylon is a real city in a location other than the city mentioned in a, whose name only is symbolic.

c. Babylon symbolizes a world system.

d. Babylon is a real city *and* symbolizes the world system of which it is the capital (e.g., 17:18*b*).

Let us look into each of these views. It is important for us to spend much time on this study in order to understand and appreciate the passage more fully. (For this discussion we are moving temporarily into the stage of interpretation; but we will return to observation shortly.)

a. Babylon, city on the Euphrates. If this view is correct, the entire city would have to be revived, between now and the end times. For, as R. K. Harrison observes, "At the present time the Baghdad to Bassorah railway line passes within a few yards of the mound that was once the most splendid city of the world."[1]

b. Babylon, symbolic name for a future world capital. Read 17:9, which locates the city ("woman") on "seven mountains." Many expositors interpret Babylon as Rome, for that city is built on seven hills. Because of Rome's history, its relation to a religion of worldwide scope, and its strategic geographical location, it is not difficult to imagine how the city could become a world capital as described in these chapters.

One weakness of interpreting Babylon only as a particular city is that it leaves unanswered the disposition of the rest of the world, who bewails her fall. For example, read 18:9-10, and observe that the evil kings are mere onlookers of Babylon's judgment.

c. Babylon represents a world system. The strength of this view is in its worldwide scope, for the last judgments of the concluding chapters of Revelation will fall upon the whole world, and not on one isolated city.

d. Babylon is a real city, capital of an evil world system, which it symbolizes. The view has the strengths of the two preceding views. All evil world systems (religious, secular, etc.) shall be judged, as Babylon is so described in these chapters. To complete the apocalyptic picture, kings, merchants and other groups appear as onlookers bewailing Babylon's fall, but really they are among

---

1. R. K. Harrison, "Babylon," in *The Zondervan Pictorial Bible Dictionary* (Grand Rapids: Zondervan, 1963), p. 93. Cf. Isa. 13:19-20 on the question of Babylon's restoration.

the fallen, for Babylon represents them as well. Also it is very reasonable to expect that such a world system would have a literal city as its central headquarters.

4. You will probably want to postpone arriving at your own interpretation of "Babylon" until after you have studied the two chapters more in detail. The questions appearing below reflect the fourth view stated above, but the answering of them should not hinder an open-minded study of the passage. (Keep in mind that the woman and Babylon are one and the same.)

5. Read chapter 17, observing every description of the woman. List these. What verses identify the woman as:

    a. of worldwide influence
    b. a political power
    c. immoral
    d. a religious power; anti-God and antigospel

6. Observe the references in this chapter to the beast. Is this the same as the beast of 13:1?

_____

_____

7. For interpretations of the political alignments and events of 17:10-16, consult various commentaries. Do not get bogged down over these difficult verses at this point in your study.

8. What does this chapter teach about the woman's destiny?

_____

Whom does God use to bring about her destruction?

_____

Does this imply that during the last times there will be ungodly systems fighting each other?

_____

Try to visualize, in its fulfillment, a context between the beast with his league of ten nations (17:12-13, 16), and the woman (17:16).

9. How does 17:18 connect chapter 17 with chapter 18?

_____

_____

10. Now read chapter 18, observing every description of the city. List these.

_____

_____

_____

What verses identify the city as:
    a. of worldwide influence
    b. a political power
    c. immoral
    d. a religious system; anti-God and antigospel
    e. a wealthy empire
11. Note the large space devoted to the material wealth of Babylon. What groups bewail her material collapse?

_____

_____

Is this really self-pity for their own plight?

_____

_____

What is the significance of the phrase "souls of men" in the list of merchandise in 18:12-13?

_____

_____

12. Make a study of the word "great" in this chapter.
13. What verses prophesy the fall of Babylon?

_____

_____

What is the symbolism of verse 21?

_____

_____

What repeated key phrase appears in 18:21-23?

_____

_____

_____

14. What is taught by the phrases "in one day" (18:8) and "in one hour" (18:10, 17, 19)?

_____

_____

15. What is the function of verse 20 in this chapter? Read the verse thus: "Rejoice over her, O heaven, and you saints and apostles and prophets, for on your behalf God has passed judgment against her" (*Berkeley*).

_____

_____

16. On the basis of your study, could it be said that Babylon is a vast world system or power, of religious, political and commercial dimensions, which will suddenly be destroyed by God in the last days?

_____

_____

III. NOTES

1. "Mystery" (17:5). It is generally agreed that this word is not part of the woman's title, but an introductory word to the title.[2] *The Berkeley Version* reads, "On her forehead a symbolic title was inscribed."

2. "Babylon the Great" (17:5). Leon Morris, commenting later about the "seven mountains" (17:9), writes:

> In the first century, Rome was a striking embodiment of what John means by Babylon. In Rome as nowhere else men could see the city of man bent on its own blasphemous way, opposing with all its might the things of God.[3]

3. "These shall hate the whore" (17:16). Ryrie comments:

> This system [harlot, Babylon] centers in Rome, includes other harlot groups, and exercises great political influence. For the first half of the tribulation she will reign unchallenged; but at the middle of the tribulation, the beast (the man of sin) will see her as a challenge to his own power and program. So with his

2. The punctuation of our Bibles is not part of the original text.
3. Leon Morris, *The Revelation of St. John*, p. 209.

league of ten nations he will destroy the harlot and set himself up to be worshiped.[4]

IV. FOR THOUGHT AND DISCUSSION

1. What characteristics of Babylon are prevalent in the world today?

_____

_____

Can you conceive of any system, power, or nation, existing today, which may eventually be the Babylon of last days?

_____

_____

2. How will it be possible that such prosperity will abound in the world during the time of chapter 18, after such destructive judgments of the seals and trumpets?

_____

_____

3. What does Revelation 17-18 teach about material wealth?

_____

_____

V. FURTHER STUDY

1. Read what these other passages teach about the satanic world system: John 12:31; 14:30; 16:11; 1 John 2:16-17; 4:3-4; 5:19; Galatians 1:4; Colossians 1:13; 2 Peter 2:20; James 4:1-4.
2. Make a topical study of "wealth" as taught by the New Testament. Are riches evil in themselves?

VI. WORD TO PONDER

"The Lamb shall overcome them: for he is Lord of lords, and King of kings" (17:14*a*).

---

4. C.C. Ryrie, _Revelation_, p. 104.

Lesson 13

Revelation 19:1–20:15

Final Judgment

The two chapters of this lesson conclude the judgment section of the book of Revelation (chaps. 6-20). God has recorded in this passage what He deems vital to reveal concerning the eternal destiny of unbelievers. It should impress every reader that so much crucial history of the end times is compacted in the short space of only thirty-six verses.

I. PREPARATION FOR STUDY

1. Chapter 19 records the climactic event of Christ's second coming to this earth (19:11-21).[1] One writer suggests that this might be the high point not only of the book of Revelation but of all history.[2] For background, read the following passages prophesying this second coming: Isaiah 63:1-6; 64:1-2; Zechariah 14:3-4; Matthew 24:27-31.

2. Review your study of 16:13-16, where reference is made to the Battle of Armageddon. When in the three series of judgments (seals, trumpets, bowls) will this battle occur?

_____

_____

Where will it be centered geographically?

_____

_____

1. As indicated earlier, this phase of His coming is to be distinguished from the first phase, called the rapture, when Christ does not come to the earth but to the air, to "catch up" His saints to heaven (1 Thess. 4:14-17).
2. John F. Walvoord, *The Revelation of Jesus Christ*, p. 274.

130

3. Review your study in Lesson 2 of the various millennial views. Keep this in mind as you study 20:1-6. Review also Chart W, showing the two last battles of world history.

II. ANALYSIS

Segments to be analyzed: 19:1-10; 19:11-21; 20:1-6; 20:7-15
Paragraph divisions: at verses 19:1, 5, 9, 11, 17; 20:1, 4, 7, 11

Many key events are described in this passage. Read the text and record its main contents under the headings shown on Chart X.

REVELATION 19:1—20:15   **Chart X**

19:1	19:11	20:1	20:7	20:11 20:15
—SONGS —MARRIAGE OF THE LAMB	—CHRIST'S RETURN TO EARTH —WAR: ARMAGEDDON	MILLENNIUM	—SATAN'S LOOSING —WAR: GOG AND MAGOG	GREAT WHITE THRONE JUDGMENT

Observe among other things the relatively short space devoted to each of the events. Is the importance of an event proportional to the space devoted to it in the Bible? In answering this, compare the fall of Babylon (36 verses) with the great white throne judgment (5 verses).

_____

_____

Analyze each of the segments, applying various methods of study used in earlier lessons. The list of questions given below is not exhaustive but touches on selected highlights of the chapters. Record as many of your studies as you can.

A. Songs, and Marriage of the Lamb (19:1-10)

Make a thorough study of the songs of verses 1-8. Contrast these with the wails of chapter 18. What is the marriage of the Lamb (v. 7)?

_____

_____

131

Who is "his wife?" (Cf. Eph. 5:23-32.)

_____

_____

Who do you think are the ones "called unto the marriage supper" (v. 9)? (Cf. Jn. 3:29.)

_____

_____

B. Christ's Second Coming and the Battle of Armageddon (19:11-21)[3]

Who is the rider on the white horse? List all the descriptions made of Him in 19:11-16. Compare this with the picture of Christ in Philippians 2:5-11.

_____

_____

_____

Why is 19:11-16 a key paragraph in Revelation?

_____

_____

_____

How is this second coming of Christ different from the rapture described in 1 Thessalonians 4:14-17?

_____

_____

_____

Observe this return of Christ to the earth takes *before* the millennium of 20:1-6, hence the term *premillennialism*.
Is much description of the war recorded in 19:17-21?

_____

_____

_____

---

3. Because of similar descriptions, the war of these verses is identified with that of 16:13-16 (and possibly 14:19-20), hence the name Armageddon.

What is the outcome of the war?

_____

_____

What is the "lake of fire burning with brimstone" (v. 20)?

_____

_____

Contrast the supper of verse 17 with the supper of verse 9.

_____

_____

C. The Millennium (20:1-6)

Observe the frequency of the phrase "thousand years."[4] Does it appear unstrained to interpret this literally? If the intention is figurative, how long a period would the phrase suggest? As you answer these two questions, be consistent with your earlier interpretations of such time phrases as "forty-two months."

_____

_____

_____

Who is the main character of verses 1-3?

_____

_____

4. This is the only Bible passage specifically mentioning the "thousand years." Walvoord correctly observes that "though problems in understanding this period persist due to the fact that there is not a complete revelation on all details, the major facts are sufficiently clear for anyone who is willing to accept the authority and accuracy of Scripture and interpret language in its ordinary sense" (p. 302). Rejection of a literal interpretation of this millennial passage is unsound if it is based on such arguments as (1) difficulties in understanding the fulfillment; (2) abuses of interpretation by some expositors; (3) the paucity of description in the New Testament. On the last-named objection, it may be noted, by way of example, that the fact of eternal heaven is not denied because not much space, proportionately, is devoted to its description in the New Testament. Likewise, the factuality of the battles of Armageddon and of Gog and Magog is not denied because hardly a verse describes the *action of each case* (see 19:20 and 20:9).

What does the phrase "bound him" (v. 2) symbolize?

_____

_____

What is the purpose of the binding? (Cf. 20:8.)

_____

_____

How does John describe the believers whom he sees, prophetically, in the Millennium? Note the two groups: those of verse 4*a*, and those of verse 4*b*.[5]

_____

_____

What references to their blessed state are made in this paragraph?

_____

_____

What is meant by "first resurrection" (v. 5), and "second death" (v. 6)?

_____

_____

Study Chart Y to understand the subordinate though important place which the Millennium holds in God's timetable of history.

D. Battle of Gog and Magog (20:7-10)

Who instigates this battle? From what source do you think he recruits his soldiers? What does the paragraph reveal as to his opponents, and the place, action, and outcome of the war? What are your impressions of this last battle of the world?

E. The Great White Throne Judgment (20:11-15)

Who is the judge? (Note: the phrase "stand before God" should read "stand before the throne.")

_____

_____

5. Some expositors see three groups in verse 4.

134

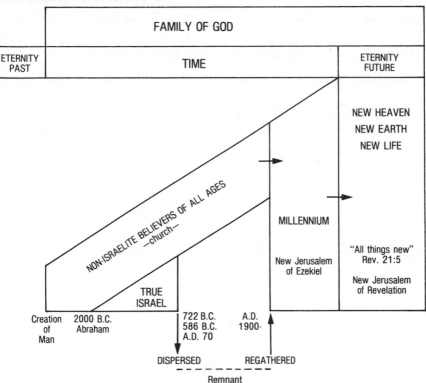

Compare the following verses concerning Christ as Judge: John 5:22; Acts 17:31; 2 Timothy 4:1; Matthew 19:28; 25:31.

_____

_____

Who are the ones judged?

_____

_____

On what basis can one say that believers will not appear at this judgment?

_____

_____

In what sense have believers already been judged?

_____

_____

What are "the books," and "another book" (v. 12)?

_____

_____

If salvation is by grace and not of works (Eph. 2:8-9), in what sense will people be judged "according to their works" (vv. 12-13)? In answering this, study carefully Ephesians 2:10, which completes the truth of Ephesians 2:8-9.

_____

_____

What is the outcome of the white throne judgment?

_____

_____

What is significant about verse 14a? (Note: "death and hell" should read "death and hades." Recall from your earlier studies the location and function of hades.)

_____

_____

How is this "second death" different from the death of unbelievers at the end of their life-span on earth?

_____

_____

_____

III. NOTES

1. "Righteousness of saints" (19:8). The phrase is better translated "righteous deeds of saints" (cf. Eph. 5:26-27).
2. "Judgment was given unto them" (20:4; cf. 1 Cor. 6:2-3; 2 Tim. 2:12).
3. "And they lived" (20:4). These are martyrs of the Tribulation period who are resurrected at the Millennium. (Cf. John 11:25 on the word "lived.")

4. "Deceive the nations" (20:8). The armies of these nations will be composed of men probably born during the Millennium who never turn to Christ for salvation, although outwardly they obey His governmental rule. At the end of the Millennium such people are easy victims of Satan's deceptions.[6]

5. "According to their works" (20:12). The record of those works may be the content of the "books" of verse 12. On judgment according to works, Ryrie comments:

> The book of life is opened only to show that no name of anyone standing before the throne is written in it. Rejection of the Saviour places men in this judgment (and excludes their names from the book of life), but works done in life prove that they deserve eternal punishment. It is almost like a final act of grace for Christ to show men that on the basis of their own records they deserve the lake of fire.[7]

IV. FOR THOUGHT AND DISCUSSION

1. What have you learned about Christ from these two chapters?

_____

_____

_____

2. Why is it necessary that all judgment be made "in righteousness" (19:11)? Read Genesis 18:25; Psalm 9:4, 8; 98:9; Isaiah 11:4; Acts 17:31; John 5:30.

_____

_____

_____

3. Why do you think the description of the Millennium in Revelation is relatively brief? Keep in mind that primarily the millennial kingdom is God's fulfillment to Israel of a restored earthly kingdom in the last days, promised through His Old Testament prophets. Chart Z illustrates this.

_____

_____

_____

6. Refer to various commentaries for further discussion of this subject.
7. C.C. Ryrie, *Revelation*, p. 117.

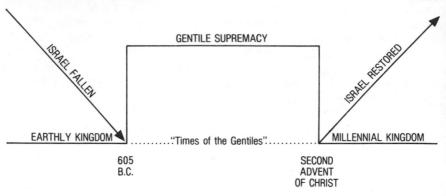

4. Apply these beautiful lines of the hymn writer Isaac Watts to the Millennium:

> Jesus shall reign where'er the sun
> Does his successive journeys run;
> His kingdom stretch from shore to shore;
> Till moons shall wax and wane no more.
>
> Let ev'ry creature rise and bring
> Peculiar honors to our King;
> Angels descend with songs again,
> And earth repeat the loud Amen!

5. Why do you think God permits Satan further opportunity to deceive people after the Millennium is over?

_____

_____

6. What is eternal death? In what sense is it a state of torment, day and night, forever and ever (20:10)?

_____

_____

Will body, soul, and spirit of an unbeliever exist for eternity, separated from the presence of God?

_____

_____

7. Meditate long over the awesome truth of 20:15.

138

8. What do you consider to be the ten most important teachings of this passage?

_____

_____

_____

_____

_____

_____

_____

V. FURTHER STUDY

1. It was pointed out in an early lesson that there is no explicit reference to the rapture of the church (1 Th. 4:14-17) in the book of Revelation. Various views are held as to where the rapture is suggested in the text. (See such locations listed on the survey Chart F.) On the basis of your study of Revelation, at what point in the book do you think the church is no longer on the earth in its present state?

_____

_____

2. Read the following Old Testament prophecies which have been identified with the Battle of Armageddon: Jeremiah 51:27-36; Joel 3:9-15; Zephaniah 3:8.
3. Most of the Bible's descriptions of the Millennium appear in the Old Testament. What will the Millennium be like, according to these prophecies: Isaiah 2:2-4; 9:6-7; 11:4-9; 30:15-33; chapters 35, 44, 49; 65:17–66:14; Jeremiah 23:5-6; Psalm 72?

_____

_____

On the prominence of Israel in the Millennium, read Ezekiel 20:34-38.[8]

---

8. For outside reading on the Millennium from the premillennial viewpoint, consult Lewis Sperry Chafer, *The Kingdom in History and Prophecy* (Westwood, N.J.: Revell, 1915); and Alva J. McClain, *The Greatness of the Kingdom* (Grand Rapids: Zondervan, 1959).

4. For outside reading on the final judgment, read Wilbur M. Smith's essay "A Righteous Judgment to Come" in *Therefore Stand*; and Harry Buis, *The Doctrine of Eternal Punishment*.[9]

VI. WORDS TO PONDER

No gospel will be preached on the day of the great white throne judgment. The irreversible, eternal judgment will have been already determined by each unbeliever during his lifetime, in rejecting Jesus as his personal Saviour.

Hear the grief-stricken voice of the rejected Saviour while He walked on this earth:

> O Jerusalem, Jerusalem, thou that killest the prophets, and stonest them which are sent unto thee, how often would I have gathered thy children together, even as a hen gathereth her chickens under her wings, and YE WOULD NOT! Behold, your house is left unto you desolate. How can ye escape the damnation of hell? (Matt. 23:37-38, 33).

9. Wilbur M. Smith, *Therefore Stand* (Grand Rapids: Baker, 1969); and Harry Buis, *The Doctrine of Eternal Punishment* (Philadelphia: Presbyterian and Reformed, 1957).

Lesson 14

Eternal Home of the Saints

We have now arrived at the final section of Revelation, the brightest chapters contained in the whole book. Any Christian reading Revelation must feel relieved to move from the long, dark catacombs of the judgment chapters (6-20) to the fresh heavenly air of John's last visions. This glorious message for believers is God's last recorded words in His holy book.

I. PREPARATION FOR STUDY

1. Take one last look at the survey Chart F, to review the contest of these concluding chapters of Revelation. Recall the message of the opening chapters of Revelation.

2. Think about the various methods the Bible uses to emphasize different truths. For example, compare the law of quantitative emphasis (the many chapters [6-20] describing judgment) with the law of contrast for emphasis (the two bright chapters of 21-22 contrasted with the preceding fifteen chapters).

3. What main truths do you expect to find in this final section about the eternal home of God's people?

_____

_____

II. ANALYSIS

Segments to be analyzed: 21:1-22:5 and 22:6-21
Paragraph divisions: at verses 21:1, 6, 9, 15, 18, 22; 22:1, 6, 7, 8, 12, 14, 16, 17, 20*a*, 20*b*, 21

A. Segment 21:1–22:5

Read the segment for general impressions. Why is the paragraph
22:1-5 included in this segment?

_____

_____

What is the main subject of the segment?

_____

_____

What is the segment's main symbol or object?

_____

_____

From your reading thus far are you inclined to think that most of
the segment should be interpreted literally or figuratively?

_____

_____

In either interpretation, what is the underlying purpose of this
passage?

_____

_____

May it be said that the passage is Revelation's description of
heaven?

_____

_____

Chart AA is a work sheet for you to record your observations as
you analyze this segment. Record key words and phrases of the
text inside the paragraph boxes; your own notes and outlines in
the margins. (One outline is shown; try making your own.)
1. *Paragraph 21:1-5*. Observe the repeated key word "new." What
new things are mentioned here? Compare Isaiah 65:17-18; 66:22; 2
Peter 3:13.

_____

_____

①

ITS APPEARANCE
IN THE
NEW UNIVERSE

21:1

"new"

②

ITS INHABITANTS

6

③

ITS DESCRIPTION
a. Structures

9

b. Dimensions

15

DESCRIPTIONS

c. Adornments

18

④

ITS EXCLUSIONS

22

"no"

27

⑤

ITS LIFE

22:1

"life"

5

143

What do you think is meant by "were passed away"? In answering this, compare 2 Peter 3:7, 10-11.

_____

_____

How does the phrase "new Jerusalem" represent both innovation and continuity?

_____

_____

Why is the picture of a city used to describe the heavenly abode of saints? (Cf. 21:3; Ps. 48:1, 8; Heb. 11:10, 16; 12:22-24; 13:14; John 14:1-3.)

_____

_____

What is taught about God in this paragraph?

_____

_____

2. _Paragraph 21:6-8._ Record on the work sheet the key truths of this paragraph. Why is verse 8 included here?

_____

_____

3. _Paragraph 21:9-14._ What important characteristics of the new Jerusalem are cited in verses 10 and 11?

_____

_____

Even in a literal interpretation of verses 12-14 the different items symbolize spiritual truths about heaven. What are your interpretations of these?

_____

_____

4. _Paragraph 21:15-17._ What is the purpose of listing the dimensions? (Note: 12,000 furlongs equal 1,500 miles; 144 cubits equal 216 feet; and the shape given in v. 16_b_ could be either a cube or a pyramid.)

_____

_____

5. *Paragraph 21:18-21*. What is the purpose of this detailed list of adornments?

_____

_____

6. *Paragraph 21:22-27*. What is the key word of this paragraph? Record on the work sheet all the things excluded from the city. Account for each exclusion.

_____

_____

_____

7. *Paragraph 22:1-5*. What references to life appear in verses 1-2?

_____

_____

What does the word "life" suggest to you in this context?

_____

_____

Compare G. Campbell Morgan's triad of heaven:
     LOVE: the one impulse
     LIGHT: the perfect guidance
     LIFE: the adequate power
What will be the believer's activities in heaven, according to verses 3-5?

_____

_____

B. Segment 22:6-21

How is this epilogue similar to the opening chapters of Revelation?

_____

_____

Observe how the words of Jesus are interspersed throughout this passage. Record those words on Chart BB. What key statement by

Jesus is repeated in the passage? To what coming does it refer? Why is it such an important word at the conclusion of Revelation?

_____

_____

_____

Analyze each paragraph carefully, recording your observations and interpretations on the work sheet.

C. A Concluding Exercise for Chapters 21-22

Starting with the interpretation that these chapters reveal selected truths about heaven, list what is taught by the chapters about the following:
1. what heaven will look like

_____

_____

2. descriptions of heaven's inhabitants

_____

_____

3. the activities of saints in heaven

_____

_____

4. heaven's bliss

_____

_____

5. descriptions of God and Christ

_____

_____

6. works of God and Christ in heaven

_____

_____

THE ANGEL, JOHN, OR OTHERS SPEAKING   CHRIST SPEAKING

6

7

8

12

14

16

17

20a

20b

21

III. NOTES

1. "No more sea" (21:1). The sea is symbolic of unrest and trouble, a divider of peoples in the world.
2. "Nations" (21:24). This word may read "Gentiles."
3. "Healing" (22:2). The Greek word means "health-giving," with the idea of serving or ministering. Note that this is another reference to *life* in the paragraph.
4. "Blessed is he" (22:7). This is the sixth of seven beatitudes in Revelation. Read the others: 1:3; 14:13; 16:15; 19:9; 20:6; 22:14.
5. "Let him be unjust still" (22:11). Walvoord says that John "does not mean that men should remain unmoved by the prophecies of this book, but rather that if the prophecies are rejected, there is no other message that will work."[1]
6. "Be with you all" (22:21). Some important ancient manuscripts read "be with all the saints."

IV. FOR THOUGHT AND DISCUSSION

1. What kind of light and brightness will the glory of God give to heaven?

_____

_____

On Christ as light, read John 1:7-9; 3:19; 8:12; 12:35-36. Compare also 1 John 1:5-7.
2. In what ways do you think you will serve God in heaven as one of His children?

_____

_____

3. What are your thoughts about 21:4?

_____

_____

4. Can human language, even that of the Bible, fully describe heaven or hell?

_____

_____

1. John F. Walvoord, *The Revelation of Jesus Christ*, p. 334.

Will the actual experience of these places be larger and more intense than any description given by the Bible?

_____

_____

V. FURTHER STUDY

1. For a study of the words translated "new" (e.g., 21:1-2), read R. C. Trench, *Synonyms of the New Testament*.[2]

2. Two other books are recommended for supplementary reading: Robert Govett, *The Apocalypse;* and Wilbur M. Smith, *The Biblical Doctrine of Heaven*.[3]

A CONCLUDING THOUGHT

The Bible opens with the story of the creation of the heavens and earth, followed by man's sin and the curse it incurred (Gen. 1-3). The Bible closes with the appearance of the new heavens and new earth, followed by a description of the saints' eternal home, where sin and curse will have no part (Rev. 21-22). In view of man's utter inability to save himself, there is only one explanation for this phenomenal restoration and salvation—and that is the grace of God. It is no wonder then that the last line of the book of Revelation spotlights this grand truth, with the benediction "The grace of our Lord Jesus Christ be with all the saints" (ASV, margin). As one writer expresses it, "Sin drove man from one garden. Grace brings man to an eternal Paradise."

2. R.C. Trench, *Synonyms of the New Testament* (Grand Rapids: Eerdmans, 1950), pp. 219-25.
3. Robert Govett, *The Apocalypse: Expounded by Scripture* (London: Chas. Thynne, 1920), pp. 549-610 (a discussion of the holy city); and Wilbur M. Smith, *The Biblical Doctrine of Heaven* (Chicago: Moody, 1968).

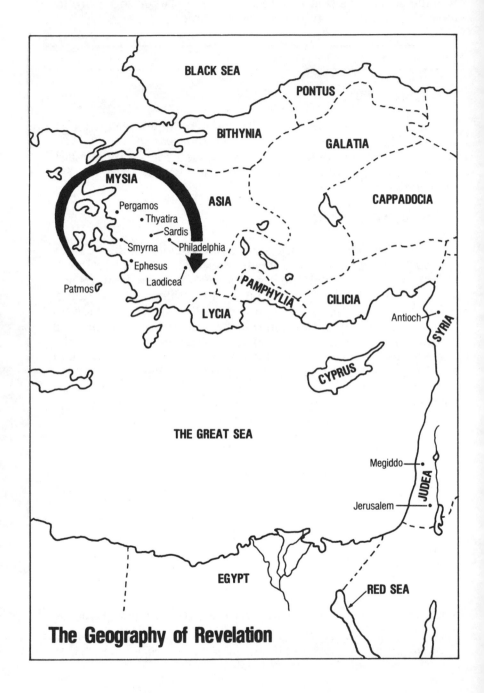

BLACK SEA

PONTUS

BITHYNIA

GALATIA

MYSIA

ASIA

CAPPADOCIA

Pergamos
• Thyatira
• Sardis
Smyrna • Philadelphia
• Ephesus
Laodicea

Patmos

PAMPHYLIA

LYCIA

CILICIA

Antioch

SYRIA

CYPRUS

THE GREAT SEA

Megiddo

JUDEA

Jerusalem

EGYPT

RED SEA

The Geography of Revelation

Bibliography

SELECTED SOURCES FOR FURTHER STUDY

Alford, Henry. *The Greek Testament*. Vol. 4. Rev. ed. Chicago: Moody, 1968.

Harrison, Norman B. *The End*. Minneapolis: Harrison, 1941. (Midtribulation viewpoint)

Lange, John Peter. *Revelation*. Grand Rapids: Zondervan, n.d.

Morris, Leon. *The Revelation of St. John*, Grand Rapids: Eerdmans, 1969.

Newell, William R. *The Book of Revelation*. Chicago: Moody, 1935.

Payne, J. Barton, *Encyclopedia of Biblical Prophecy*. New York: Harper & Row, 1973.

Robertson, A.T. *Word Pictures in the New Testament*. Vol. 6. New York: Harper, 1933.

Ryrie, Charles Caldwell. *Revelation*. Everyman's Bible Commentary. Chicago: Moody, 1968.

Sauer, Erich. *From Eternity to Eternity*. Grand Rapids: Eerdmans, 1954.

Scott, Walter. *Exposition of the Revelation of Jesus Christ*. London: Pickering & Inglis, n.d.

Seiss, J.A. *The Apocalypse*. Grand Rapids: Zondervan, 1865.

Smith, Wilbur M. "Revelation." In *The Wycliffe Bible Commentary*, ed. C.F. Pfeiffer and E.F. Harrison. Chicago: Moody, 1962.

Swete, H.B. *The Apocalypse of St. John*. Grand Rapids: Eerdmans, 1951.

Tenney, Merrill C. *Interpreting Revelation*. Grand Rapids: Eerdmans, 1957.

Unger, Merrill F. *Unger's Bible Handbook*. Chicago: Moody, 1966.

Vincent, Marvin R. *Word Studies in the New Testament*. Vol. 2. Grand Rapids: Eerdmans, 1946.

Walvoord, John F. *The Revelation of Jesus Christ*. Chicago: Moody, 1966.